WALLACE STEVENS

Wallace Stevens was born [in] Harvard, he turned his ba[ck on] poetry with a career in the [insurance business. Although they made a] modest impression at the ti[me, his first collection, *Harmonium*] (1923), would become a lan[dmark in modern] American poetry, and would be followed by such works as *Ideas of Order* (1935), *The Man with the Blue Guitar and Other Poems* (1937), *Notes toward a Supreme Fiction* (1942), *Transport to Summer* (1947) and *The Necessary Angel* (1951). Wallace Stevens died in 1955; a collection of poems, plays and prose appeared in *Opus Posthumous* (1957).

John Burnside is a poet and author and was born in Dunfermline in 1955. He has published ten volumes of poems, including *The Asylum Dance* (2000), winner of the Whitbread Poetry Award, and most recently *Gift Songs*, shortlisted for the 2007 Forward Poetry Prize. A *Selected Poems* was published in 2006; his latest novel is *The Devil's Footprints*. He lives in Fife.

IN THE POET-TO-POET SERIES

W. H. AUDEN – Poems selected by John Fuller
WILLIAM BARNES – Poems selected by Andrew Motion
JOHN BERRYMAN – Poems selected by Michael Hofmann
JOHN BETJEMAN – Poems selected by Hugo Williams
ROBERT BROWNING – Poems selected by Douglas Dunn
ROBERT BURNS – Poems selected by Don Paterson
LORD BYRON – Poems selected by Paul Muldoon
THOMAS CAMPION – Poems selected by Charles Simic
JOHN CLARE – Poems selected by Paul Farley
SAMUEL TAYLOR COLERIDGE – Poems selected by James
   Fenton
HART CRANE – Poems selected by Maurice Riordan
EMILY DICKINSON – Poems selected by Ted Hughes
KEITH DOUGLAS – Poems selected by Ted Hughes
JOHN DRYDEN – Poems selected by Charles Tomlinson
ALLEN GINSBERG – Poems selected by Mark Ford
THOM GUNN – Poems selected by August Kleinzahler
THOMAS HARDY – Poems selected by Tom Paulin
GEORGE HERBERT – Poems selected by Jo Shapcott
GERARD MANLEY HOPKINS – Poems selected by
   John Stammers
A. E. HOUSMAN – Poems selected by Alan Hollinghurst
TED HUGHES – Poems selected by Simon Armitage
JOHN KEATS – Poems selected by Andrew Motion
D. H. LAWRENCE – Poems selected by Tom Paulin
ROBERT LOWELL – Poems selected by Michael Hofmann
LOUIS MACNEICE – Poems selected by Michael Longley
WILFRED OWEN – Poems selected by Jon Stallworthy
SYLVIA PLATH – Poems selected by Ted Hughes
EZRA POUND – Poems selected by Thom Gunn
JOHN SKELTON – Poems selected by Anthony Thwaite
WALLACE STEVENS – Poems selected by John Burnside
JONATHAN SWIFT – Poems selected by Derek Mahon
ALFRED, LORD TENNYSON – Poems selected by Mick Imlah
DYLAN THOMAS – Poems selected by Derek Mahon
WILLIAM WORDSWORTH – Poems selected by Seamus Heaney
THOMAS WYATT – Poems selected by Alice Oswald
W. B. YEATS – Poems selected by Seamus Heaney

WALLACE STEVENS
Poems selected by JOHN BURNSIDE

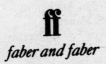

faber and faber

First published in 2008
by Faber and Faber Limited
3 Queen Square London WC1N 3AU

Typeset by RefineCatch Ltd, Bungay, Suffolk
Printed in England by CPI Bookmarque, Croydon

A CIP record for this book
is available from the British Library

ISBN 978-0-571-23793-7

10 9 8 7 6 5 4 3 2 1

Contents

Introduction vii

The Snow Man 3
A High-Toned Old Christian Woman 4
The Emperor of Ice-Cream 5
Disillusionment of Ten O'Clock 6
Sunday Morning 7
To the One of Fictive Music 11
Peter Quince at the Clavier 13
Thirteen Ways of Looking at a Blackbird 16
Anatomy of Monotony 19
Sad Strains of a Gay Waltz 20
The Idea of Order at Key West 21
The American Sublime 23
Botanist on Alp (No. 1) 24
Botanist on Alp (No. 2) 25
Evening Without Angels 26
The Man with the Blue Guitar 28
Parochial Theme 44
A Rabbit as King of the Ghosts 45
The Blue Buildings in the Summer Air 46
On the Adequacy of Landscape 48
Of Bright & Blue Birds & the Gala Sun 49
Asides on the Oboe 50
Dutch Graves in Bucks County 52
No Possum, No Sop, No Taters 55
Crude Foyer 56
Esthétique du Mal 57
The House Was Quiet and the World Was Calm 69
The Dove in the Belly 70
Credences of Summer 71
Notes Toward a Supreme Fiction 77
What We See Is What We Think 100

An Ordinary Evening in New Haven 101
A Quiet Normal Life 121
Final Soliloquy of the Interior Paramour 122
The Rock 123
The Dove in Spring 124
The Planet on the Table 127
Not Ideas About the Thing But the Thing Itself 128
Of Mere Being 129
A Clear Day and No Memories 130

Introduction

'I have no life except in poetry.' At first sight, this would appear to be a surprising, even rather a stark, declaration, coming as it does from the vice-president of a leading Hartford insurance company, a well-read man with wide-ranging interests, aZuent enough to have paintings and fine wine shipped from France when he felt so inclined, a physically and intellectually impos- ing individual, with an obvious air of money and expensive taste ('money is a kind of poetry', he once said), a man some- what dandyish in his dress, yet characterised by Harriet Monroe as possessing a 'quiet power' and seen by many as the model for the visiting poet – 'John D. Rockefeller drenched in attar of roses' – in Mary McCarthy's novel *The Groves of Academe*. 'I have no life except in poetry.' No doubt his family would have been dismayed to read such a statement, while his colleagues, whom he kept carefully segregated from his literary associates, would have been suitably bemused; yet, in the almost unique case of Wallace Stevens, it is a statement, perhaps one should say an admission, that can *almost* be taken at face value. 'I have no life except in poetry.' It sounds like something a wan Romantic might utter from his sad garret, and under those circumstances would be nothing more than a pose, an affectation; spoken by a well-to-do, slightly plump, somewhat dandyish executive, it is an idea that can only be seen as an example, and as a challenge.

'I have no life except in poetry.' The line comes from *Adagia*, probably the most intriguing and beautiful set of meditations on the discipline of poetry written in English. It is a line that rings true for many poets because, in sharp contrast to public obsession with biographical details (an attempt to make the poet into that more manageable commodity, a *celebrity*), 'the life' of the poet is of very limited interest, other than as gossip or as extremely dubious 'background information'. We may say of Stevens that he was born in 1879 and died in 1955; for most of his life he lived and worked in Hartford, Connecticut, as an insurance lawyer; after a long courtship (five years, a long engagement even for the time, but then Stevens was, as he himself says, an 'indefatigable procrastinator'), he married Elsie Kachel, an attractive but rather frail woman seven years his junior; the marriage seems to have been unsatisfying and restrictive on Stevens, whose smoking and fondness for wine was frowned upon, while plans to create a library for his extensive book collection in the eleven-room house he shared with Elsie were never realised. A cautious perfectionist, Stevens delayed publishing his first collection for many years; at the very end of his life, when he had achieved considerable fame, he declined an offer to become the Charles Eliot Norton Professor of poetry at Harvard because, as Frank Kermode records in his admirably brief account of the life in his short study of Stevens's work (published in 1960), 'he felt that a year away from his office would make retirement inevitable'. He was seventy-five.

The rest is anecdote. My own favourite is also related by Kermode:

> There is a story, told me by a very distinguished American writer, concerning an English philosopher of the greatest distinction, who met Stevens at a lecture in Harvard and asked if he might call at Hartford; the answer was a blunt and unqualified 'No', with nothing to palliate the old man's discomfiture. Stevens was a very big, formidable man, though gentle in manner; he had obviously long assumed that one makes decisions and that these decisions then take effect. He had enforced that privacy which it was in his power to preserve, and which was the voluntary equivalent of the alienation regarded as necessary for other poets; but perhaps it was a condition to be maintained by a certain degree of egotism, perhaps it involved a few rather shocking gestures of this kind.

Perhaps. My feeling, however (as a writer who worked for ten years in a similar, though less lofty business environment), is that Stevens needed such hard and fast (and essentially inexplicable) rules in order to sustain a more than usually compartmentalised double life. It is a life that every poet leads to a greater or lesser extent. Or rather, it is the discipline that poets must master, in order to sustain that mysterious entity, a *private life*, and Stevens was more keenly aware of this discipline than most. Even in the early years, when he was just beginning to find his mature voice, he could write to his impatient fiancée:

> I certainly do not exist from nine to six, when I am at the office . . . There is no everyday Wallace, apart from the one at work – and that one is tedious. – At night I strut my individual state one more.

It is this 'individual state', this private life, that allows us to catch the fleeting and tentative glimpses of the wider order that makes for actual poems, and that process of seeing and making order of things – what Stevens calls 'the daily necessity of getting the world right' – is, and should be allowed to remain, a mysterious one, part alchemy, part conjuring trick, a process that begins and ends in that individual state. When Stevens says he has no life except in poetry he is making a clear distinction between the 'tedious' and the 'individual state'; he wants to set something apart from the world of casual prurience and gossip, to make of the poem a separate entity in itself, an entity that exemplifies a supreme, but entirely provisional, achievement of order.

Our fondness for gossip is not the only reason for Stevens's relative neglect on this side of the Atlantic, however. His 'image' was initially difficult for a British audience, for a number of reasons. To begin with, as Kermode notes, Stevens's reputation was not helped by early critics – Empson, for example – pointing out that he was 'dandyish, American and rich'. Yet that is only part of the problem. A poet who could make the suggestion that money 'is a kind of poetry' might not be expected to go down well in a post-war Britain plagued by rationing, and Stevens compounded the sin by being the most Francophone of Americans, a reader not only of the Symbolists and Baudelaire, but also of the great French philosophers. Add to this that he was, like William Carlos Williams and Marianne Moore, unashamedly *American* in his sensibility, and his reduction to the status of Imagist, conjuring up poems about snowmen and blackbirds, is complete, in spite of the fact that his master works – his most American works – are the long, discursive sequences of his later period. What America needed, in the first decades of the last century, was a new idiom, a new aesthetic, that was not in any way beholden to Europe and, especially, to England, and Stevens was one of the first poets to light out for the Territory, making work that was startlingly different from anything that had been written before, either in America or anywhere else. In Stevens's hands, poetry becomes a daring, sometimes breathtaking investigation into the nature of reality, a subject to which he returns again and again, because, in his view, 'Poetry increases the feeling for reality' – and an increased feeling for reality is, in itself, oddly subversive in an age where the gloss of appearances is so important – the semblance of truth, the trappings of celebrity – and experience is continuously repackaged as a mere commodity. Thus, in a letter to Delmore Schwartz, Stevens outlines what he thinks of as poetry's function in maintaining the liberty of the individual in a political culture:

> It seems that poetic order is potentially as significant as philosophic order. Accordingly, it is natural to project the idea of a theory of poetry that would be pretty much the same thing as a theory of the world based on a coordination of the poetic aspects of the world. Such an idea completely changes the significance of poetry. It does what poetry itself does, that is to say, it leads to a fresh conception of the world ... Many sensitive readers of poetry, without being mystics or romantics or metaphysicians, feel that there probably is available in reality something accessible through a theory of poetry which would make a profound difference in our sense of the world.

And he continues:

One's interest is, however, an interest in life and in reality. From this point of view it is easy to say that the basic meaning of literary effort, and, therefore, of poetry, is with reference to life and reality and not with reference to politics. The basic meaning of the effort of any man to record his experience as poet is to produce poetry, not politics. The poet must stand or fall by poetry. In the conflict between the poet and the politician the chief honor the poet can hope for is that of remaining himself.

Around the same time, he revisits this idea, in a letter to Harry Duncan:

Today, in America, all roles yield to that of the politician.

The role of the poet may be fixed by contrasting it to that of the politician. The poet absorbs the general life: the public life. The politician is absorbed by it. The poet is individual. The politician is general. It is the personal in the poet that is the origin of his poetry . . . If people are to become dependent on poetry for any of the fundamental satisfactions, poetry must have an increasingly intellectual scope and power. This is a time for the highest poetry. We never understood the world less than we do now nor, as we understand it, liked it less. We never wanted to understand it more or needed to like it more. These are the intense compulsions that challenge the poet as the appreciatory creator of values and beliefs. That, finally, states the problem.

The appreciatory creator of values and beliefs: Stevens begins to sound like Shelley and his 'unacknowledged legislators' here; yet his is an entirely modern sensibility and it quickly becomes obvious, reading beyond the anthologised work, and especially on close reading of the great extended sequences of the later collections, that here is a poet who is responding, in an utterly original and quite astonishing way, to the demands made by twentieth-century philosophy and science for a new way of thinking about the world. When Stevens says:

A man and a woman
Are one.
A man and a woman and a blackbird
Are one

I cannot help but think again of Hannah Arendt's contention that 'metaphor is the means by which the oneness of the world is poetically brought about', and, while it is certainly something of a stretch – and a limitation – to see Stevens as some kind of 'nature poet', we can say that his work is suffused with a new way of thinking about the world, a way of thinking that a contemporary reader might be forgiven for calling ecological. By which I mean: a sense of the earth itself as the ground of our existence, a sense of the oneness Arendt recognises as predating the descriptive energies of language. Stevens himself is keenly aware of this: 'Poetry means not the language of poetry but the thing itself, wherever it may be found,' he says, in a note to Henry Church, dated 1940. This idea may seem surprising, in the light of the sheer delight Stevens takes in language, and language games, especially in the early work, but it is entirely consistent with his vision. What Stevens is after is reality and, even if reality can only be arrived at through the creation of a 'necessary fiction', reality – *the world* – is poetry's principal concern. But what world? We live in the *as if*, in a world that we imagine, we inhabit what we have determined to be the necessary fiction and this is the origin of both our sometimes tragic freedom and our immense responsibility. The challenge is clearly stated in the opening lines of 'Asides on the Oboe':

The prologues are over. It is a question, now,
Of final belief. So, say that final belief
Must be in a fiction. It is time to choose.

So it is that Stevens sees poetry as having a fundamental role in the creation of reality, for it is through poetry that we approach the necessary (or even the *supreme*) fiction. Poetry is how we make a world; poetry is, quite literally, the song of the earth.

Other poets have claimed as much, before and since, and the original poet – in Western European culture, at least – is the shaman Orpheus, who could conjure up new animals merely by singing. Poetry is how we imagine the world and, as such, is not merely a political, but an ecological and ontological activity. What makes Stevens's poetry distinctive in this respect, however, is that his vision is always of a world in its most diverse, complex and subtle state: nobody knows better than Stevens that there is as much darkness in the song of the earth as there is light, as much grief as there is joy.

Making a selection from Stevens's work is, therefore, more than usually difficult, mostly because one comes to think of it, on repeated reading, as a single fabric, a lifelong discipline. Critics have always disliked it when poets seem to repeat themselves, when they appear to have nothing 'new' to say – yet surely it is in the nature of philosophical poetry to go back, to think again, to continue the dialogue with the natural order. It seems to me that there is no fault in returning to the same questions again and again; on the contrary, such a tendency means that we are capable of something more than mere novelty – love, say, or passion, or perhaps just a dedication to asking the *right* questions as well as we can. After all, what matters does not change that much. What we care about is our place in the world, how we live with others, how we face violence and fear, how we love, how we approach death, what we think of as 'the Good'. Stevens certainly returned to familiar subject matter in his later work – and often produced work that outshines the early work upon which, to date, his reputation depends – yet that does not simplify the anthologist's task in making a selection. Indeed, the opposite holds true: one wants to choose everything, to retain that sense of a single fabric, and of an extraordinarily keen and disciplined mind at work over a long and thoughtful lifetime.

Omissions are not accidents, as Marianne Moore said, but most of the omissions here are much regretted. I chose, however, to leave out some poems that can be found elsewhere without too much of a search, and to bring to the fore others, mostly from the later work, that do not, as yet, seem to me to have enjoyed their proper place in the sun. My principal hope is that this selection will prompt a general reader to seek out the *Collected Poems* (and also the wonderful prose works and letters, which must stand as some of the finest prose writing by any poet anywhere) and read on, especially into the later work, and the great poem sequences. Far too many of us still see Stevens as the poet of 'Thirteen Ways of Looking at a Blackbird' and 'The Snow Man' but, as fine as these are, he was much more than that. I hope the great sequences included here – twentieth-century masterpieces like 'Esthétique du Mal', 'An Ordinary Evening in New Haven' and, of course, 'Notes Toward a Supreme Fiction' – will send readers to those marvellous sequences I was obliged to pass over, just as I hope that a reading of a wonderful late short poem like 'Final Soliloquy of the Interior Paramour' or 'The Planet on the Table' will serve as reminder that this poet's later oeuvre is at least as vital and rewarding as anything he wrote in the Twenties and Thirties.

JOHN BURNSIDE

WALLACE STEVENS

The Snow Man

One must have a mind of winter
To regard the frost and the boughs
Of the pine-trees crusted with snow;

And have been cold a long time
To behold the junipers shagged with ice,
The spruces rough in the distant glitter

Of the January sun; and not to think
Of any misery in the sound of the wind,
In the sound of a few leaves,

Which is the sound of the land
Full of the same wind
That is blowing in the same bare place

For the listener, who listens in the snow,
And, nothing himself, beholds
Nothing that is not there and the nothing that is.

A High-Toned Old Christian Woman

Poetry is the supreme fiction, madame.
Take the moral law and make a nave of it
And from the nave build haunted heaven. Thus,
The conscience is converted into palms,
Like windy citherns hankering for hymns.
We agree in principle. That's clear. But take
The opposing law and make a peristyle,
And from the peristyle project a masque
Beyond the planets. Thus, our bawdiness,
Unpurged by epitaph, indulged at last,
Is equally converted into palms,
Squiggling like saxophones. And palm for palm,
Madame, we are where we began. Allow,
Therefore, that in the planetary scene
Your disaffected flagellants, well-stuffed,
Smacking their muzzy bellies in parade,
Proud of such novelties of the sublime,
Such tink and tank and tunk-a-tunk-tunk,
May, merely may, madame, whip from themselves
A jovial hullabaloo among the spheres.
This will make widows wince. But fictive things
Wink as they will. Wink most when widows wince.

The Emperor of Ice-Cream

Call the roller of big cigars,
The muscular one, and bid him whip
In kitchen cups concupiscent curds.
Let the wenches dawdle in such dress
As they are used to wear, and let the boys
Bring flowers in last month's newspapers.
Let be be finale of seem.
The only emperor is the emperor of ice-cream.

Take from the dresser of deal,
Lacking the three glass knobs, that sheet
On which she embroidered fantails once
And spread it so as to cover her face.
If her horny feet protrude, they come
To show how cold she is, and dumb.
Let the lamp affix its beam.
The only emperor is the emperor of ice-cream.

Disillusionment of Ten O'Clock

The houses are haunted
By white night-gowns.
None are green,
Or purple with green rings,
Or green with yellow rings,
Or yellow with blue rings.
None of them are strange,
With socks of lace
And beaded ceintures.
People are not going
To dream of baboons and periwinkles.
Only, here and there, an old sailor,
Drunk and asleep in his boots,
Catches tigers
In red weather.

Sunday Morning

I

Complacencies of the peignoir, and late
Coffee and oranges in a sunny chair,
And the green freedom of a cockatoo
Upon a rug mingle to dissipate
The holy hush of ancient sacrifice.
She dreams a little, and she feels the dark
Encroachment of that old catastrophe,
As a calm darkens among water-lights.
The pungent oranges and bright, green wings
Seem things in some procession of the dead,
Winding across wide water, without sound.
The day is like wide water, without sound,
Stilled for the passing of her dreaming feet
Over the seas, to silent Palestine,
Dominion of the blood and sepulchre.

II

Why should she give her bounty to the dead?
What is divinity if it can come
Only in silent shadows and in dreams?
Shall she not find in comforts of the sun,
In pungent fruit and bright, green wings, or else
In any balm or beauty of the earth,
Things to be cherished like the thought of heaven?
Divinity must live within herself:
Passions of rain, or moods in falling snow;
Grievings in loneliness, or unsubdued
Elations when the forest blooms; gusty
Emotions on wet roads on autumn nights;
All pleasures and all pains, remembering
The bough of summer and the winter branch.
These are the measures destined for her soul.

III

Jove in the clouds had his inhuman birth.
No mother suckled him, no sweet land gave
Large-mannered motions to his mythy mind.
He moved among us, as a muttering king,
Magnificent, would move among his hinds,
Until our blood, commingling, virginal,
With heaven, brought such requital to desire
The very hinds discerned it, in a star.
Shall our blood fail? Or shall it come to be
The blood of paradise? And shall the earth
Seem all of paradise that we shall know?
The sky will be much friendlier then than now,
A part of labor and a part of pain,
And next in glory to enduring love,
Not this dividing and indifferent blue.

IV

She says, 'I am content when wakened birds,
Before they fly, test the reality
Of misty fields, by their sweet questionings;
But when the birds are gone, and their warm fields
Return no more, where, then, is paradise?'
There is not any haunt of prophesy,
Nor any old chimera of the grave,
Neither the golden underground, nor isle
Melodious, where spirits gat them home,
Nor visionary south, nor cloudy palm
Remote on heaven's hill, that has endured
As April's green endures; or will endure
Like her remembrance of awakened birds,
Or her desire for June and evening, tipped
By the consummation of the swallow's wings.

V

She says, 'But in contentment I still feel
The need of some imperishable bliss.'
Death is the mother of beauty; hence from her,
Alone, shall come fulfilment to our dreams
And our desires. Although she strews the leaves
Of sure obliteration on our paths,
The path sick sorrow took, the many paths
Where triumph rang its brassy phrase, or love
Whispered a little out of tenderness,
She makes the willow shiver in the sun
For maidens who were wont to sit and gaze
Upon the grass, relinquished to their feet.
She causes boys to pile new plums and pears
On disregarded plate. The maidens taste
And stray impassioned in the littering leaves.

VI

Is there no change of death in paradise?
Does ripe fruit never fall? Or do the boughs
Hang always heavy in that perfect sky,
Unchanging, yet so like our perishing earth,
With rivers like our own that seek for seas
They never find, the same receding shores
That never touch with inarticulate pang?
Why set the pear upon those river-banks
Or spice the shores with odors of the plum?
Alas, that they should wear our colors there,
The silken weavings of our afternoons,
And pick the strings of our insipid lutes!
Death is the mother of beauty, mystical,
Within whose burning bosom we devise
Our earthly mothers waiting, sleeplessly.

Supple and turbulent, a ring of men
Shall chant in orgy on a summer morn
Their boisterous devotion to the sun,
Not as a god, but as a god might be,
Naked among them, like a savage source.
Their chant shall be a chant of paradise,
Out of their blood, returning to the sky;
And in their chant shall enter, voice by voice,
The windy lake wherein their lord delights,
The trees, like serafin, and echoing hills,
That choir among themselves long afterward.
They shall know well the heavenly fellowship
Of men that perish and of summer morn.
And whence they came and whither they shall go
The dew upon their feet shall manifest.

She hears, upon that water without sound,
A voice that cries, 'The tomb in Palestine
Is not the porch of spirits lingering.
It is the grave of Jesus, where he lay.'
We live in an old chaos of the sun,
Or old dependency of day and night,
Or island solitude, unsponsored, free,
Of that wide water, inescapable.
Deer walk upon our mountains, and the quail
Whistle about us their spontaneous cries;
Sweet berries ripen in the wilderness;
And, in the isolation of the sky,
At evening, casual flocks of pigeons make
Ambiguous undulations as they sink,
Downward to darkness, on extended wings.

To the One of Fictive Music

Sister and mother and diviner love,
And of the sisterhood of the living dead
Most near, most clear, and of the clearest bloom,
And of the fragrant mothers the most dear
And queen, and of diviner love the day
And flame and summer and sweet fire, no thread
Of cloudy silver sprinkles in your gown
Its venom of renown, and on your head
No crown is simpler than the simple hair.

Now, of the music summoned by the birth
That separates us from the wind and sea,
Yet leaves us in them, until earth becomes,
By being so much of the things we are,
Gross effigy and simulacrum, none
Gives motion to perfection more serene
Than yours, out of our imperfections wrought,
Most rare, or ever of more kindred air
In the laborious weaving that you wear.

For so retentive of themselves are men
That music is intensest which proclaims
The near, the clear, and vaunts the clearest bloom,
And of all vigils musing the obscure,
That apprehends the most which sees and names,
As in your name, an image that is sure,
Among the arrant spices of the sun,
O bough and bush and scented vine, in whom
We give ourselves our likest issuance.

Yet not too like, yet not so like to be
Too near, too clear, saving a little to endow
Our feigning with the strange unlike, whence springs
The difference that heavenly pity brings.

For this, musician, in your girdle fixed
Bear other perfumes. On your pale head wear
A band entwining, set with fatal stones.
Unreal, give back to us what once you gave:
The imagination that we spurned and crave.

Peter Quince at the Clavier

I

Just as my fingers on these keys
Make music, so the self-same sounds
On my spirit make a music, too.

Music is feeling, then, not sound;
And thus it is that what I feel,
Here in this room, desiring you,

Thinking of your blue-shadowed silk,
Is music. It is like the strain
Waked in the elders by Susanna;

Of a green evening, clear and warm,
She bathed in her still garden, while
The red-eyed elders, watching, felt

The basses of their beings throb
In witching chords, and their thin blood
Pulse pizzicati of Hosanna.

II

In the green water, clear and warm,
Susanna lay.
She searched
The touch of springs,
And found
Concealed imaginings.
She sighed,
For so much melody.

Upon the bank, she stood
In the cool

Of spent emotions.
She felt, among the leaves,
The dew
Of old devotions.

She walked upon the grass,
Still quavering.
The winds were like her maids,
On timid feet,
Fetching her woven scarves,
Yet wavering.

A breath upon her hand
Muted the night.
She turned –
A cymbal crashed,
And roaring horns.

III

Soon, with a noise like tambourines,
Came her attendant Byzantines.

They wondered why Susanna cried
Against the elders by her side;

And as they whispered, the refrain
Was like a willow swept by rain.

Anon, their lamps' uplifted flame
Revealed Susanna and her shame.

And then, the simpering Byzantines
Fled, with a noise like tambourines.

IV

Beauty is momentary in the mind –
The fitful tracing of a portal;
But in the flesh it is immortal.

The body dies; the body's beauty lives.
So evenings die, in their green going,
A wave, interminably flowing.
So gardens die, their meek breath scenting
The cowl of winter, done repenting.
So maidens die, to the auroral
Celebration of a maiden's choral.

Susanna's music touched the bawdy strings
Of those white elders; but, escaping,
Left only Death's ironic scraping.
Now, in its immortality, it plays
On the clear viol of her memory,
And makes a constant sacrament of praise.

Thirteen Ways of Looking at a Blackbird

I

Among twenty snowy mountains,
The only moving thing
Was the eye of the black bird.

II

I was of three minds,
Like a tree
In which there are three blackbirds.

III

The blackbird whirled in the autumn winds.
It was a small part of the pantomime.

IV

A man and a woman
Are one.
A man and a woman and a blackbird
Are one.

V

I do not know which to prefer,
The beauty of inflections
Or the beauty of innuendoes,
The blackbird whistling
Or just after.

VI

Icicles filled the long window
With barbaric glass.

The shadow of the blackbird
Crossed it, to and fro.
The mood
Traced in the shadow
An indecipherable cause.

VII

O thin men of Haddam,
Why do you imagine golden birds?
Do you not see how the blackbird
Walks around the feet
Of the women about you?

VIII

I know noble accents
And lucid, inescapable rhythms;
But I know, too,
That the blackbird is involved
In what I know.

IX

When the blackbird flew out of sight,
It marked the edge
Of one of many circles.

X

At the sight of blackbirds
Flying in a green light,
Even the bawds of euphony
Would cry out sharply.

XI

He rode over Connecticut
In a glass coach.

Once, a fear pierced him,
In that he mistook
The shadow of his equipage
For blackbirds.

XII

The river is moving.
The blackbird must be flying.

XIII

It was evening all afternoon.
It was snowing
And it was going to snow.
The blackbird sat
In the cedar-limbs.

Anatomy of Monotony

I

If from the earth we came, it was an earth
That bore us as a part of all the things
It breeds and that was lewder than it is.
Our nature is her nature. Hence it comes,
Since by our nature we grow old, earth grows
The same. We parallel the mother's death.
She walks an autumn ampler than the wind
Cries up for us and colder than the frost
Pricks in our spirits at the summer's end,
And over the bare spaces of our skies
She sees a barer sky that does not bend.

II

The body walks forth naked in the sun
And, out of tenderness or grief, the sun
Gives comfort, so that other bodies come,
Twinning our phantasy and our device,
And apt in versatile motion, touch and sound
To make the body covetous in desire
Of the still finer, more implacable chords.
So be it. Yet the spaciousness and light
In which the body walks and is deceived,
Falls from that fatal and that barer sky,
And this the spirit sees and is aggrieved.

Sad Strains of a Gay Waltz

The truth is that there comes a time
When we can mourn no more over music
That is so much motionless sound.

There comes a time when the waltz
Is no longer a mode of desire, a mode
Of revealing desire and is empty of shadows.

Too many waltzes have ended. And then
There's that mountain-minded Hoon,
For whom desire was never that of the waltz,

Who found all form and order in solitude,
For whom the shapes were never the figures of men.
Now, for him, his forms have vanished.

There is order in neither sea nor sun.
The shapes have lost their glistening.
There are these sudden mobs of men,

These sudden clouds of faces and arms,
An immense suppression, freed,
These voices crying without knowing for what,

Except to be happy, without knowing how,
Imposing forms they cannot describe,
Requiring order beyond their speech.

Too many waltzes have ended. Yet the shapes
For which the voices cry, these, too, may be
Modes of desire, modes of revealing desire.

Too many waltzes – The epic of disbelief
Blares oftener and soon, will soon be constant.
Some harmonious skeptic soon in a skeptical music

Will unite these figures of men and their shapes
Will glisten again with motion, the music
Will be motion and full of shadows.

The Idea of Order at Key West

She sang beyond the genius of the sea.
The water never formed to mind or voice,
Like a body wholly body, fluttering
Its empty sleeves; and yet its mimic motion
Made constant cry, caused constantly a cry,
That was not ours although we understood,
Inhuman, of the veritable ocean.

The sea was not a mask. No more was she.
The song and water were not medleyed sound
Even if what she sang was what she heard,
Since what she sang was uttered word by word.
It may be that in all her phrases stirred
The grinding water and the gasping wind;
But it was she and not the sea we heard.

For she was the maker of the song she sang.
The ever-hooded, tragic-gestured sea
Was merely a place by which she walked to sing.
Whose spirit is this? we said, because we knew
It was the spirit that we sought and knew
That we should ask this often as she sang.

If it was only the dark voice of the sea
That rose, or even colored by many waves;
If it was only the outer voice of sky
And cloud, of the sunken coral water-walled,
However clear, it would have been deep air,
The heaving speech of air, a summer sound
Repeated in a summer without end
And sound alone. But it was more than that,
More even than her voice, and ours, among
The meaningless plungings of water and the wind,
Theatrical distances, bronze shadows heaped

On high horizons, mountainous atmospheres
Of sky and sea.

                    It was her voice that made
The sky acutest at its vanishing.
She measured to the hour its solitude.
She was the single artificer of the world
In which she sang. And when she sang, the sea,
Whatever self it had, became the self
That was her song, for she was the maker. Then we,
As we beheld her striding there alone,
Knew that there never was a world for her
Except the one she sang and, singing, made.

Ramon Fernandez, tell me, if you know,
Why, when the singing ended and we turned
Toward the town, tell why the glassy lights,
The lights in the fishing boats at anchor there,
As the night descended, tilting in the air,
Mastered the night and portioned out the sea,
Fixing emblazoned zones and fiery poles,
Arranging, deepening, enchanting night.

Oh! Blessed rage for order, pale Ramon,
The maker's rage to order words of the sea,
Words of the fragrant portals, dimly-starred,
And of ourselves and of our origins,
In ghostlier demarcations, keener sounds.

The American Sublime

How does one stand
To behold the sublime,
To confront the mockers,
The mickey mockers
And plated pairs?

When General Jackson
Posed for his statue
He knew how one feels.
Shall a man go barefoot
Blinking and blank?

But how does one feel?
One grows used to the weather,
The landscape and that;
And the sublime comes down
To the spirit itself,

The spirit and space,
The empty spirit
In vacant space.
What wine does one drink?
What bread does one eat?

Botanist on Alp (No. 1)

Panoramas are not what they used to be.
Claude has been dead a long time
And apostrophes are forbidden on the funicular.
Marx has ruined Nature,
For the moment.

For myself, I live by leaves,
So that corridors of clouds,
Corridors of cloudy thoughts,
Seem pretty much one:
I don't know what.

But in Claude how near one was
(In a world that was resting on pillars,
That was seen through arches)
To the central composition,
The essential theme.

What composition is there in all this:
Stockholm slender in a slender light,
An adriatic *riva* rising,
Statues and stars,
Without a theme?

The pillars are prostrate, the arches are haggard,
The hotel is boarded and bare.
Yet the panorama of despair
Cannot be the specialty
Of this ecstatic air.

Botanist on Alp (No. 2)

The crosses on the convent roofs
Gleam sharply as the sun comes up.

What's down below is in the past
Like last night's crickets, far below.

And what's above is in the past
As sure as all the angels are.

Why should the future leap the clouds
The bays of heaven, brighted, blued?

Chant, O ye faithful, in your paths
The poem of long celestial death;

For who could tolerate the earth
Without that poem, or without

An earthier one, tum, tum-ti-tum,
As of those crosses, glittering,

And merely of their glittering,
A mirror of a mere delight?

Evening Without Angels

the great interests of man: air and light, the joy of having a
body, the voluptuousness of looking.   MARIO ROSSI

Why seraphim like lutanists arranged
Above the trees? And why the poet as
Eternal *chef d'orchestre*?

                  Air is air.
Its vacancy glitters round us everywhere.
Its sounds are not angelic syllables
But our unfashioned spirits realized
More sharply in more furious selves.

                And light
That fosters seraphim and is to them
Coiffeur of haloes, fecund jeweller –
Was the sun concoct for angels or for men?
Sad men made angels of the sun, and of
The moon they made their own attendant ghosts,
Which led them back to angels, after death.

Let this be clear that we are men of sun
And men of day and never of pointed night,
Men that repeat antiquest sounds of air
In an accord of repetitions. Yet,
If we repeat, it is because the wind
Encircling us, speaks always with our speech.

Light, too, encrusts us making visible
The motions of the mind and giving form
To moodiest nothings, as, desire for day
Accomplished in the immensely flashing East,
Desire for rest, in that descending sea
Of dark, which in its very darkening
Is rest and silence spreading into sleep.

. . . Evening, when the measure skips a beat
And then another, one by one, and all
To a seething minor swiftly modulate.
Bare night is best. Bare earth is best. Bare, bare,
Except for our own houses, huddled low
Beneath the arches and their spangled air,
Beneath the rhapsodies of fire and fire,
Where the voice that is in us makes a true response,
Where the voice that is great within us rises up,
As we stand gazing at the rounded moon.

The Man with the Blue Guitar

I

The man bent over his guitar,
A shearsman of sorts. The day was green.

They said, 'You have a blue guitar,
You do not play things as they are.'

The man replied, 'Things as they are
Are changed upon the blue guitar.'

And they said then, 'But play, you must,
A tune beyond us, yet ourselves,

A tune upon the blue guitar
Of things exactly as they are.'

II

I cannot bring a world quite round,
Although I patch it as I can.

I sing a hero's head, large eye
And bearded bronze, but not a man,

Although I patch him as I can
And reach through him almost to man.

If to serenade almost to man
Is to miss, by that, things as they are,

Say that it is the serenade
Of a man that plays a blue guitar.

III

Ah, but to play man number one,
To drive the dagger in his heart,

To lay his brain upon the board
And pick the acrid colors out,

To nail his thought across the door,
Its wings spread wide to rain and snow,

To strike his living hi and ho,
To tick it, tock it, turn it true,

To bang it from a savage blue,
Jangling the metal of the strings . . .

IV

So that's life, then: things as they are?
It picks its way on the blue guitar.

A million people on one string?
And all their manner in the thing,

And all their manner, right and wrong,
And all their manner, weak and strong?

The feelings crazily, craftily call,
Like a buzzing of flies in autumn air,

And that's life, then: things as they are,
This buzzing of the blue guitar.

V

Do not speak to us of the greatness of poetry,
Of the torches wisping in the underground,

Of the structure of vaults upon a point of light.
There are no shadows in our sun,

Day is desire and night is sleep.
There are no shadows anywhere.

The earth, for us, is flat and bare.
There are no shadows. Poetry

Exceeding music must take the place
Of empty heaven and its hymns,

Ourselves in poetry must take their place,
Even in the chattering of your guitar.

VI

A tune beyond us as we are,
Yet nothing changed by the blue guitar;

Ourselves in the tune as if in space,
Yet nothing changed, except the place

Of things as they are and only the place
As you play them, on the blue guitar,

Placed, so, beyond the compass of change,
Perceived in a final atmosphere;

For a moment final, in the way
The thinking of art seems final when

The thinking of god is smoky dew.
The tune is space. The blue guitar

Becomes the place of things as they are,
A composing of senses of the guitar.

VII

It is the sun that shares our works.
The moon shares nothing. It is a sea.

When shall I come to say of the sun,
It is a sea; it shares nothing;

The sun no longer shares our works
And the earth is alive with creeping men,

Mechanical beetles never quite warm?
And shall I then stand in the sun, as now

I stand in the moon, and call it good,
The immaculate, the merciful good,

Detached from us, from things as they are?
Not to be part of the sun? To stand

Remote and call it merciful?
The strings are cold on the blue guitar.

VIII

The vivid, florid, turgid sky,
The drenching thunder rolling by,

The morning deluged still by night,
The clouds tumultuously bright

And the feeling heavy in cold chords
Struggling toward impassioned choirs,

Crying among the clouds, enraged
By gold antagonists in air –

I know my lazy, leaden twang
Is like the reason in a storm;

And yet it brings the storm to bear.
I twang it out and leave it there.

IX

And the color, the overcast blue
Of the air, in which the blue guitar

Is a form, described but difficult,
And I am merely a shadow hunched

Above the arrowy, still strings,
The maker of a thing yet to be made;

The color like a thought that grows
Out of a mood, the tragic robe

Of the actor, half his gesture, half
His speech, the dress of his meaning, silk

Sodden with his melancholy words,
The weather of his stage, himself.

X

Raise reddest columns. Toll a bell
And clap the hollows full of tin.

Throw papers in the streets, the wills
Of the dead, majestic in their seals.

And the beautiful trombones – behold
The approach of him whom none believes,

Whom all believe that all believe,
A pagan in a varnished car.

Roll a drum upon the blue guitar.
Lean from the steeple. Cry aloud,

'Here am I, my adversary, that
Confront you, hoo-ing the slick trombones,

Yet with a petty misery
At heart, a petty misery,

Ever the prelude to your end,
The touch that topples men and rock.'

XI

Slowly the ivy on the stones
Becomes the stones. Women become

The cities, children become the fields
And men in waves become the sea.

It is the chord that falsifies.
The sea returns upon the men,

The fields entrap the children, brick
Is a weed and all the flies are caught,

Wingless and withered, but living alive.
The discord merely magnifies.

Deeper within the belly's dark
Of time, time grows upon the rock.

XII

Tom-tom, c'est moi. The blue guitar
And I are one. The orchestra

Fills the high hall with shuZing men
High as the hall. The whirling noise

Of a multitude dwindles, all said,
To his breath that lies awake at night.

I know that timid breathing. Where
Do I begin and end? And where,

As I strum the thing, do I pick up
That which momentously declares

Itself not to be I and yet
Must be. It could be nothing else.

XIII

The pale intrusions into blue
Are corrupting pallors . . . ay di mi,

Blue buds or pitchy blooms. Be content –
Expansions, diffusions – content to be

The unspotted imbecile revery,
The heraldic center of the world

Of blue, blue sleek with a hundred chins,
The amorist Adjective aflame . . .

XIV

First one beam, then another, then
A thousand are radiant in the sky.

Each is both star and orb; and day
Is the riches of their atmosphere.

The sea appends its tattery hues.
The shores are banks of muZing mist.

One says a German chandelier –
A candle is enough to light the world.

It makes it clear. Even at noon
It glistens in essential dark.

At night, it lights the fruit and wine,
The book and bread, things as they are,

In a chiaroscuro where
One sits and plays the blue guitar.

XV

Is this picture of Picasso's, this 'hoard
Of destructions', a picture of ourselves,

Now, an image of our society?
Do I sit, deformed, a naked egg,

Catching at Good-bye, harvest moon,
Without seeing the harvest or the moon?

Things as they are have been destroyed.
Have I? Am I a man that is dead

At a table on which the food is cold?
Is my thought a memory, not alive?

Is the spot on the floor, there, wine or blood
And whichever it may be, is it mine?

XVI

The earth is not earth but a stone,
Not the mother that held men as they fell

But stone, but like a stone, no: not
The mother, but an oppressor, but like

An oppressor that grudges them their death,
As it grudges the living that they live.

To live in war, to live at war,
To chop the sullen psaltery,

To improve the sewers in Jerusalem,
To electrify the nimbuses –

Place honey on the altars and die,
You lovers that are bitter at heart.

XVII

The person has a mould. But not
Its animal. The angelic ones

Speak of the soul, the mind. It is
An animal. The blue guitar –

On that its claws propound, its fangs
Articulate its desert days.

The blue guitar a mould? That shell?
Well, after all, the north wind blows

A horn, on which its victory
Is a worm composing in a straw.

XVIII

A dream (to call it a dream) in which
I can believe, in face of the object,

A dream no longer a dream, a thing,
Of things as they are, as the blue guitar

After long strumming on certain nights
Gives the touch of the senses, not of the hand,

But the very senses as they touch
The wind-gloss. Or as daylight comes,

Like light in a mirroring of cliffs,
Rising upward from a sea of ex.

XIX

That I may reduce the monster to
Myself, and then may be myself

In face of the monster, be more than part
Of it, more than the monstrous player of

One of its monstrous lutes, not be
Alone, but reduce the monster and be,

Two things, the two together as one,
And play of the monster and of myself,

Or better not of myself at all,
But of that as its intelligence,

Being the lion in the lute
Before the lion locked in stone.

XX

What is there in life except one's ideas,
Good air, good friend, what is there in life?

Is it ideas that I believe?
Good air, my only friend, believe,

Believe would be a brother full
Of love, believe would be a friend,

Friendlier than my only friend,
Good air. Poor pale, poor pale guitar . . .

XXI

A substitute for all the gods:
This self, not that gold self aloft,

Alone, one's shadow magnified,
Lord of the body, looking down,

As now and called most high,
The shadow of Chocorua

In an immenser heaven, aloft,
Alone, lord of the land and lord

Of the men that live in the land, high lord.
One's self and the mountains of one's land,

Without shadows, without magnificence,
The flesh, the bone, the dirt, the stone.

XXII

Poetry is the subject of the poem,
From this the poem issues and

To this returns. Between the two,
Between issue and return, there is

An absence in reality,
Things as they are. Or so we say.

But are these separate? Is it
An absence for the poem, which acquires

Its true appearances there, sun's green,
Cloud's red, earth feeling, sky that thinks?

From these it takes. Perhaps it gives,
In the universal intercourse.

XXIII

A few final solutions, like a duet
With the undertaker: a voice in the clouds,

Another on earth, the one a voice
Of ether, the other smelling of drink,

The voice of ether prevailing, the swell
Of the undertaker's song in the snow

Apostrophizing wreaths, the voice
In the clouds serene and final, next

The grunted breath serene and final,
The imagined and the real, thought

And the truth, Dichtung und Wahrheit, all
Confusion solved, as in a refrain

One keeps on playing year by year,
Concerning the nature of things as they are.

XXIV

A poem like a missal found
In the mud, a missal for that young man,

That scholar hungriest for that book,
The very book, or, less, a page

Or, at the least, a phrase, that phrase,
A hawk of life, that latined phrase:

To know; a missal for brooding-sight.
To meet that hawk's eye and to flinch

Not at the eye but at the joy of it.
I play. But this is what I think.

He held the world upon his nose
And this-a-way he gave a fling.

His robes and symbols, ai-yi-yi —
And that-a-way he twirled the thing.

Sombre as fir-trees, liquid cats
Moved in the grass without a sound.

They did not know the grass went round.
The cats had cats and the grass turned gray

And the world had worlds, ai, this-a-way:
The grass turned green and the grass turned gray.

And the nose is eternal, that-a-way.
Things as they were, things as they are,

Things as they will be by and by . . .
A fat thumb beats out ai-yi-yi.

XXVI

The world washed in his imagination,
The world was a shore, whether sound or form

Or light, the relic of farewells,
Rock, of valedictory echoings,

To which his imagination returned,
From which it sped, a bar in space,

Sand heaped in the clouds, giant that fought
Against the murderous alphabet:

The swarm of thoughts, the swarm of dreams
Of inaccessible Utopia.

A mountainous music always seemed
To be falling and to be passing away.

XXVII

It is the sea that whitens the roof.
The sea drifts through the winter air.

It is the sea that the north wind makes.
The sea is in the falling snow.

This gloom is the darkness of the sea.
Geographers and philosophers,

Regard. But for that salty cup,
But for the icicles on the eaves –

The sea is a form of ridicule.
The iceberg settings satirize

The demon that cannot be himself,
That tours to shift the shifting scene.

XXVIII

I am a native in this world
And think in it as a native thinks,

Gesu, not native of a mind
Thinking the thoughts I call my own,

Native, a native in the world
And like a native think in it.

It could not be a mind, the wave
In which the watery grasses flow

And yet are fixed as a photograph,
The wind in which the dead leaves blow.

Here I inhale profounder strength
And as I am, I speak and move

And things are as I think they are
And say they are on the blue guitar.

XXIX

In the cathedral, I sat there, and read,
Alone, a lean Review and said,

'These degustations in the vaults
Oppose the past and the festival.

What is beyond the cathedral, outside,
Balances with nuptial song.

So it is to sit and to balance things
To and to and to the point of still,

To say of one mask it is like,
To say of another it is like,

To know that the balance does not quite rest,
That the mask is strange, however like.'

The shapes are wrong and the sounds are false.
The bells are the bellowings of bulls.

Yet Franciscan don was never more
Himself than in this fertile glass.

XXX

From this I shall evolve a man.
This is his essence: the old fantoche

Hanging his shawl upon the wind,
Like something on the stage, puffed out,

His strutting studied through centuries.
At last, in spite of his manner, his eye

A-cock at the cross-piece on a pole
Supporting heavy cables, slung

Through Oxidia, banal suburb,
One-half of all its installments paid.

Dew-dapper clapper-traps, blazing
From crusty stacks above machines.

Ecce, Oxidia is the seed
Dropped out of this amber-ember pod,

Oxidia is the soot of fire,
Oxidia is Olympia.

XXXI

How long and late the pheasant sleeps . . .
The employer and employee contend,

Combat, compose their droll affair.
The bubbling sun will bubble up,

Spring sparkle and the cock-bird shriek.
The employer and employee will hear

And continue their affair. The shriek
Will rack the thickets. There is no place,

Here, for the lark fixed in the mind,
In the museum of the sky. The cock

Will claw sleep. Morning is not sun,
It is this posture of the nerves,

As if a blunted player clutched
The nuances of the blue guitar.

It must be this rhapsody or none,
The rhapsody of things as they are.

XXXII

Throw away the lights, the definitions,
And say of what you see in the dark

That it is this or that it is that,
But do not use the rotted names.

How should you walk in that space and know
Nothing of the madness of space,

Nothing of its jocular procreations?
Throw the lights away. Nothing must stand

Between you and the shapes you take
When the crust of shape has been destroyed.

You as you are? You are yourself.
The blue guitar surprises you.

XXXIII

That generation's dream, aviled
In the mud, in Monday's dirty light,

That's it, the only dream they knew,
Time in its final block, not time

To come, a wrangling of two dreams.
Here is the bread of time to come,

Here is its actual stone. The bread
Will be our bread, the stone will be

Our bed and we shall sleep by night.
We shall forget by day, except

The moments when we choose to play
The imagined pine, the imagined jay.

Parochial Theme

Long-tailed ponies go nosing the pine-lands,
Ponies of Parisians shooting on the hill.

The wind blows. In the wind, the voices
Have shapes that are not yet fully themselves,

Are sounds blown by a blower into shapes,
The blower squeezed to the thinnest *mi* of falsetto.

The hunters run to and fro. The heavy trees,
The grunting, shuZing branches, the robust,

The nocturnal, the antique, the blue-green pines
Deepen the feelings to inhuman depths.

These are the forest. This health is holy,
This halloo, halloo, halloo heard over the cries

Of those for whom a square room is a fire,
Of those whom the statues torture and keep down.

This health is holy, this descant of a self,
This barbarous chanting of what is strong, this blare.

But salvation here? What about the rattle of sticks
On tins and boxes? What about horses eaten by wind?

When spring comes and the skeletons of the hunters
Stretch themselves to rest in their first summer's sun,

The spring will have a health of its own, with none
Of autumn's halloo in its hair. So that closely, then,

Health follows after health. Salvation there:
There's no such thing as life; or if there is,

It is faster than the weather, faster than
Any character. It is more than any scene:

Of the guillotine or of any glamorous hanging.
Piece the world together, boys, but not with your hands.

A Rabbit as King of the Ghosts

The difficulty to think at the end of day,
When the shapeless shadow covers the sun
And nothing is left except light on your fur –

There was the cat slopping its milk all day,
Fat cat, red tongue, green mind, white milk
And August the most peaceful month.

To be, in the grass, in the peacefullest time,
Without that monument of cat,
The cat forgotten in the moon;

And to feel that the light is a rabbit-light,
In which everything is meant for you
And nothing need be explained;

Then there is nothing to think of. It comes of itself;
And east rushes west and west rushes down,
No matter. The grass is full

And full of yourself. The trees around are for you,
The whole of the wideness of night is for you,
A self that touches all edges,

You become a self that fills the four corners of night.
The red cat hides away in the fur-light
And there you are humped high, humped up,

You are humped higher and higher, black as stone –
You sit with your head like a carving in space
And the little green cat is a bug in the grass.

The Blue Buildings in the Summer Air

I

Cotton Mather died when I was a boy. The books
He read, all day, all night and all the nights,
Had got him nowhere. There was always the doubt,
That made him preach the louder, long for a church
In which his voice would roll its cadences,
After the sermon, to quiet that mouse in the wall.

II

Over wooden Boston, the sparkling Byzantine
Was everything that Cotton Mather was
And more. Yet the eminent thunder from the mouse,
The grinding in the arches of the church,
The plaster dropping, even dripping, down,
The mouse, the moss, the woman on the shore . . .

III

If the mouse should swallow the steeple, in its time . . .
It was a theologian's needle, much
Too sharp for that. The shore, the sea, the sun,
Their brilliance through the lattices, crippled
The chandeliers, their morning glazes spread
In opal blobs along the walls and floor.

IV

Look down now, Cotton Mather, from the blank.
Was heaven where you thought? It must be there.
It must be where you think it is, in the light
On bed-clothes, in an apple on a plate.
It is the honey-comb of the seeing man.
It is the leaf the bird brings back to the boat.

v

Go, mouse, go nibble at Lenin in his tomb.
Are you not le plus pur, you ancient one?

Cut summer down to find the honey-comb.
You are one . . . Go hunt for honey in his hair.
You are one of the not-numberable mice
Searching all day, all night, for the honey-comb.

On the Adequacy of Landscape

The little owl flew through the night,
As if the people in the air
Were frightened and he frightened them,
By being there,

The people that turned off and came
To avoid the bright, discursive wings,
To avoid the hap-hallow hallow-ho
Of central things,

Nor in their empty hearts to feel
The blood-red redness of the sun,
To shrink to an insensible,
Small oblivion,

Beyond the keenest diamond day
Of people sensible to pain,
When cocks wake, clawing at their beds
To be again,

And who, for that, turn toward the cocks
And toward the start of day and trees
And light behind the body of night
And sun, as if these

Were what they are, the sharpest sun:
The sharpest self, the sensible range,
The extent of what they are, the strength
That they exchange,

So that he that suffers most desires
The red bird most and the strongest sky –
Not the people in the air that hear
The little owl fly.

Of Bright & Blue Birds & the Gala Sun

Some things, niño, some things are like this,
That instantly and in themselves they are gay
And you and I are such things, O most miserable . . .

For a moment they are gay and are a part
Of an element, the exactest element for us,
In which we pronounce joy like a word of our own.

It is there, being imperfect, and with these things
And erudite in happiness, with nothing learned,
That we are joyously ourselves and we think

Without the labor of thought, in that element,
And we feel, in a way apart, for a moment, as if
There was a bright *scienza* outside of ourselves,

A gaiety that is being, not merely knowing,
The will to be and to be total in belief,
Provoking a laughter, an agreement, by surprise.

Asides on the Oboe

The prologues are over. It is a question, now,
Of final belief. So, say that final belief
Must be in a fiction. It is time to choose.

I

That obsolete fiction of the wide river in
An empty land; the gods that Boucher killed;
And the metal heroes that time granulates –
The philosophers' man alone still walks in dew,
Still by the sea-side mutters milky lines
Concerning an immaculate imagery.
If you say on the hautboy man is not enough,
Can never stand as god, is ever wrong
In the end, however naked, tall, there is still
The impossible possible philosophers' man,

The man who has had the time to think enough,
The central man, the human globe, responsive
As a mirror with a voice, the man of glass,
Who in a million diamonds sums us up.

II

He is the transparence of the place in which
He is and in his poems we find peace.
He sets this peddler's pie and cries in summer,
The glass man, cold and numbered, dewily cries,
"Thou art not August unless I make thee so."
Clandestine steps upon imagined stairs
Climb through the night, because his cuckoos call.

III

One year, death and war prevented the jasmine scent
And the jasmine islands were bloody martyrdoms.

How was it then with the central man? Did we
Find peace? We found the sum of men. We found,
If we found the central evil, the central good.
We buried the fallen without jasmine crowns.
There was nothing he did not suffer, no; nor we.

It was not as if the jasmine ever returned.
But we and the diamond globe at last were one.
We had always been partly one. It was as we came
To see him, that we were wholly one, as we heard
Him chanting for those buried in their blood,
In the jasmine haunted forests, that we knew
The glass man, without external reference.

Dutch Graves in Bucks County

Angry men and furious machines
Swarm from the little blue of the horizon
To the great blue of the middle height.
Men scatter throughout clouds.
The wheels are too large for any noise.

And you, my semblables, in sooty residence
Tap skeleton drums inaudibly.

There are shouts and voices.
There are men shuZing on foot in air.
Men are moving and marching
And shuZing lightly, with the heavy lightness
Of those that are marching, many together.

And you, my semblables – the old flag of Holland
Flutters in tiny darkness.

There are circles of weapons in the sun.
The air attends the brightened guns,
As if sounds were forming
Out of themselves, a saying,
An expressive on-dit, a profession.

And you, my semblables, are doubly killed
To be buried in desert and deserted earth.

The flags are natures newly found.
Rifles grow sharper on the sight.
There is a rumble of autumnal marching,
From which no soft sleeve relieves us.
Fate is the present desperado.

And you, my semblables, are crusts that lie
In the shrivellings of your time and place.

There is a battering of the drums. The bugles
Cry loudly, cry out in the powerful heart.

A force gathers that will cry loudlier
Than the most metal music, loudlier,
Like an instinctive incantation.

And you, my semblables, in the total
Of remembrance share nothing of ourselves.

An end must come in a merciles triumph,
An end of evil in a profounder logic,
In a peace that is more than a refuge,
In the will of what is common to all men,
Spelled from spent living and spent dying.

And you, my semblables, in gaffer-green,
Know that the past is not part of the present.

There were other soldiers, other people,
Men came as the sun comes, early children
And late wanderers creeping under the barb of night,
Year, year and year, defeated at last and lost
In an ignorance of sleep with nothing won.

And you, my semblables, know that this time
Is not an early time that has grown late.

But these are not those rusted armies.
There are the lewdest and the lustiest,
The hullaballoo of health and have,
The much too many disinherited
In a storm of torn-up testaments.

And you, my semblables, know that your children
Are not your children, not your selves.

Who are the mossy cronies muttering,
Monsters antique and haggard with past thought?
What is this crackling of voices in the mind,
This pitter-patter of archaic freedom,
Of the thousands of freedoms except our own?

And you, my semblables, whose ecstasy
Was the glory of heaven in the wilderness –

Freedom is like a man who kills himself
Each night, an incessant butcher, whose knife
Grows sharp in blood. The armies kill themselves,
And in their blood an ancient evil dies –
The action of incorrigible tragedy.

And you, my semblables, behold in blindness
That a new glory of new men assembles.

This is the pit of torment that placid end
Should be illusion, that the mobs of birth
Avoid our stale perfections, seeking out
Their own, waiting until we go
To picnic in the ruins that we leave.

So that the stars, my semblables, chimeres,
Shine on the very living of those alive.

These violent marchers of the present,
Rumbling along the autumnal horizon,
Under the arches, over the arches, in arcs
Of a chaos composed in more than order,
March toward a generation's centre.

Time was not wasted in your subtle temples.
No: nor divergence made too steep to follow down.

No Possum, No Sop, No Taters

He is not here, the old sun,
As absent as if we were asleep.

The field is frozen. The leaves are dry.
Bad is final in this light.

In this bleak air the broken stalks
Have arms without hands. They have trunks

Without legs or, for that, without heads.
They have heads in which a captive cry

Is merely the moving of a tongue.
Snow sparkles like eyesight falling to earth,

Like seeing fallen brightly away.
The leaves hop, scraping on the ground.

It is deep January. The sky is hard.
The stalks are firmly rooted in ice.

It is in this solitude, a syllable,
Out of these gawky flitterings,

Intones its single emptiness,
The savagest hollow of winter-sound.

It is here, in this bad, that we reach
The last purity of the knowledge of good.

The crow looks rusty as he rises up.
Bright is the malice in his eye . . .

One joins him there for company,
But at a distance, in another tree.

Crude Foyer

Thought is false happiness: the idea
That merely by thinking one can,
Or may, penetrate, not may,
But can, that one is sure to be able –

That there lies at the end of thought
A foyer of the spirit in a landscape
Of the mind, in which we sit
And wear humanity's bleak crown;

In which we read the critique of paradise
And say it is the work
Of a comedian, this critique;
In which we sit and breathe

An innocence of an absolute,
False happiness, since we know that we use
Only the eye as faculty, that the mind
Is the eye, and that this landscape of the mind

Is a landscape only of the eye; and that
We are ignorant men incapable
Of the least, minor, vital metaphor, content,
At last, there, when it turns out to be here.

Esthétique du Mal

I

He was at Naples writing letters home
And, between his letters, reading paragraphs
On the sublime. Vesuvius had groaned
For a month. It was pleasant to be sitting there,
While the sultriest fulgurations, flickering,
Cast corners in the glass. He could describe
The terror of the sound because the sound
Was ancient. He tried to remember the phrases: pain
Audible at noon, pain torturing itself,
Pain killing pain on the very point of pain.
The volcano trembled in another ether,
As the body trembles at the end of life.

It was almost time for lunch. Pain is human.
There were roses in the cool café. His book
Made sure of the most correct catastrophe.
Except for us, Vesuvius might consume
In solid fire the utmost earth and know
No pain (ignoring the cocks that crow us up
To die). This is a part of the sublime
From which we shrink. And yet, except for us,
The total past felt nothing when destroyed.

II

At a town in which acacias grew, he lay
On his balcony at night. Warblings became
Too dark, too far, too much the accents of
Afflicted sleep, too much the syllables
That would form themselves, in time, and communicate
The intelligence of his despair, express
What meditation never quite achieved.

The moon rose up as if it had escaped
His meditation. It evaded his mind.
It was part of a supremacy always
Above him. The moon was always free from him,
As night was free from him. The shadow touched
Or merely seemed to touch him as he spoke
A kind of elegy he found in space:

It is pain that is indifferent to the sky
In spite of the yellow of the acacias, the scent
Of them in the air still hanging heavily
In the hoary-hanging night. It does not regard
This freedom, this supremacy, and in
Its own hallucination never sees
How that which rejects it saves it in the end.

III

His firm stanzas hang like hives in hell
Or what hell was, since now both heaven and hell
Are one, and here, O terra infidel.

The fault lies with an over-human god,
Who by sympathy has made himself a man
And is not to be distinguished, when we cry

Because we suffer, our oldest parent, peer
Of the populace of the heart, the reddest lord,
Who has gone before us in experience.

If only he would not pity us so much,
Weaken our fate, relieve us of woe both great
And small, a constant fellow of destiny,

A too, too human god, self-pity's kin
And uncourageous genesis . . . It seems
As if the health of the world might be enough.

It seems as if the honey of common summer
Might be enough, as if the golden combs
Were part of a sustenance itself enough,

As if hell, so modified, had disappeared,
As if pain, no longer satanic mimicry,
Could be borne, as if we were sure to find our way.

IV

Livre de Toutes Sortes de Fleurs D'Après Nature.
All sorts of flowers. That's the sentimentalist.
When B. sat down at the piano and made
A transparence in which we heard music, made music,
In which we heard transparent sounds, did he play
All sorts of notes? Or did he play only one
In an ecstasy of its associates,
Variations in the tones of a single sound,
The last, or sounds so single they seemed one?

And then that Spaniard of the rose, itself
Hot-hooded and dark-blooded, rescued the rose
From nature, each time he saw it, making it,
As he saw it, exist in his own especial eye.
Can we conceive of him as rescuing less,
As muffing the mistress for her several maids,
As foregoing the nakedest passion for barefoot
Philandering? . . . The genius of misfortune
Is not a sentimentalist. He is
That evil, that evil in the self, from which
In desperate hallow, rugged gesture, fault
Falls out on everything: the genius of
The mind, which is our being, wrong and wrong,
The genius of the body, which is our world,
Spent in the false engagements of the mind.

V

Softly let all true sympathizers come,
Without the inventions of sorrow or the sob
Beyond invention. Within what we permit,
Within the actual, the warm, the near,
So great a unity, that it is bliss,
Ties us to those we love. For this familiar,
This brother even in the father's eye,
This brother half-spoken in the mother's throat
And these regalia, these things disclosed,
These nebulous brilliancies in the smallest look
Of the being's deepest darling, we forego
Lament, willingly forfeit the ai-ai

Of parades in the obscurer selvages.
Be near me, come closer, touch my hand, phrases
Compounded of dear relation, spoken twice,
Once by the lips, once by the services
Of central sense, these minutiae mean more
Than clouds, benevolences, distant heads.
These are within what we permit, in-bar
Exquisite in poverty against the suns
Of ex-bar, in-bar retaining attributes
With which we vested, once, the golden forms
And the damasked memory of the golden forms
And ex-bar's flower and fire of the festivals
Of the damasked memory of the golden forms,
Before we were wholly human and knew ourselves.

The sun, in clownish yellow, but not a clown,
Brings the day to perfection and then fails. He dwells
In a consummate prime, yet still desires
A further consummation. For the lunar month
He makes the tenderest research, intent

On a transmutation which, when seen, appears
To be askew. And space is filled with his
Rejected years. A big bird pecks at him
For food. The big bird's boney appetite
Is as insatiable as the sun's. The bird
Rose from an imperfection of its own
To feed on the yellow bloom of the yellow fruit
Dropped down from turquoise leaves. In the landscape of
The sun, its grossest appetite becomes less gross,
Yet, when corrected, has its curious lapses,
Its glitters, its divinations of serene
Indulgence out of all celestial sight.

The sun is the country wherever he is. The bird
In the brightest landscape downwardly revolves
Disdaining each astringent ripening,
Evading the point of redness, not content
To repose in an hour or season or long era
Of the country colors crowding against it, since
The yellow grassman's mind is still immense,
Still promises perfections cast away.

VII

How red the rose that is the soldier's wound,
The wounds of many soldiers, the wounds of all
The soldiers that have fallen, red in blood,
The soldier of time grown deathless in great size.

A mountain in which no ease is ever found,
Unless indifference to deeper death
Is ease, stands in the dark, a shadows' hill,
And there the soldier of time has deathless rest.

Concentric circles of shadows, motionless
Of their own part, yet moving on the wind,
Form mystical convolutions in the sleep
Of time's red soldier deathless on his bed.

The shadows of his fellows ring him round
In the high night, the summer breathes for them
Its fragrance, a heavy somnolence, and for him,
For the soldier of time, it breathes a summer sleep,

In which his wound is good because life was.
No part of him was ever part of death.
A woman smoothes her forehead with her hand
And the soldier of time lies calm beneath that stroke.

VIII

The death of Satan was a tragedy
For the imagination. A capital
Negation destroyed him in his tenement
And, with him, many blue phenomena.
It was not the end he had foreseen. He knew
That his revenge created filial
Revenges. And negation was eccentric.
It had nothing of the Julian thunder-cloud:
The assassin flash and rumble . . . He was denied.
Phantoms, what have you left? What underground?
What place in which to be is not enough
To be? You go, poor phantoms, without place
Like silver in the sheathing of the sight,
As the eye closes . . . How cold the vacancy
When the phantoms are gone and the shaken realist
First sees reality. The mortal no
Has its emptiness and tragic expirations.
The tragedy, however, may have begun,
Again, in the imagination's new beginning,
In the yes of the realist spoken because he must
Say yes, spoken because under every no
Lay a passion for yes that had never been broken.

Panic in the face of the moon – round effendi
Or the phosphored sleep in which he walks abroad
Or the majolica dish heaped up with phosphored fruit
That he sends ahead, out of the goodness of his heart,
To anyone that comes – panic, because
The moon is no longer these nor anything
And nothing is left but comic ugliness
Or a lustred nothingness. Effendi, he
That has lost the folly of the moon becomes
The prince of the proverbs of pure poverty.
To lose sensibility, to see what one sees,
As if sight had not its own miraculous thrift,
To hear only what one hears, on meaning alone,
As if the paradise of meaning ceased
To be paradise, it is this to be destitute.
This is the sky divested of its fountains.
Here in the west indifferent crickets chant
Through our indifferent crises. Yet we require
Another chant, an incantation, as in
Another and later genesis, music
That buffets the shapes of its possible halcyon
Against the haggardie . . . A loud, large water
Bubbles up in the night and drowns the crickets' sound.
It is a declaration, a primitive ecstasy,
Truth's favors sonorously exhibited.

X

He had studied the nostalgias. In these
He sought the most grossly maternal, the creature
Who most fecundly assuaged him, the softest
Woman with a vague moustache and not the mauve
Maman. His anima liked its animal
And liked it unsubjugated, so that home
Was a return to birth, a being born

Again in the savagest severity,
Desiring fiercely, the child of a mother fierce
In his body, fiercer in his mind, merciless
To accomplish the truth in his intelligence.
It is true there were other mothers, singular
In form, lovers of heaven and earth, she-wolves
And forest tigresses and women mixed
With the sea. These were fantastic. There were homes
Like things submerged with their englutted sounds,
That were never wholly still. The softest woman,
Because she is as she was, reality,
The gross, the fecund, proved him against the touch
Of impersonal pain. Reality explained.
It was the last nostalgia: that he
Should understand. That he might suffer or that
He might die was the innocence of living, if life
Itself was innocent. To say that it was
Disentangled him from sleek ensolacings.

XI

Life is a bitter aspic. We are not
At the centre of a diamond. At dawn,
The paratroopers fall and as they fall
They mow the lawn. A vessel sinks in waves
Of people, as big bell-billows from its bell
Bell-bellow in the village steeple. Violets,
Great tufts, spring up from buried houses
Of poor, dishonest people, for whom the steeple,
Long since, rang out farewell, farewell, farewell.

Natives of poverty, children of malheur,
The gaiety of language is our seigneur.

A man of bitter appetite despises
A well-made scene in which paratroopers
Select adieux; and he despises this:

A ship that rolls on a confected ocean,
The weather pink, the wind in motion; and this:
A steeple that tip-tops the classic sun's
Arrangements; and the violets' exhumo.

The tongue caresses these exacerbations.
They press it as epicure, distinguishing
Themselves from its essential savor,
Like hunger that feeds on its own hungriness.

XII

He disposes the world in categories, thus:
The peopled and the unpeopled. In both, he is
Alone. But in the peopled world, there is,
Besides the people, his knowledge of them. In
The unpeopled, there is his knowledge of himself.
Which is more desperate in the moments when
The will demands that what he thinks be true?

Is it himself in them that he knows or they
In him? If it is himself in them, they have
No secret from him. If it is they in him,
He has no secret from them. This knowledge
Of them and of himself destroys both worlds,
Except when he escapes from it. To be
Alone is not to know them or himself.

This creates a third world without knowledge,
In which no one peers, in which the will makes no
Demands. It accepts whatever is as true,
Including pain, which, otherwise, is false.
In the third world, then, there is no pain. Yes, but
What lover has one in such rocks, what woman,
However known, at the centre of the heart?

XIII

It may be that one life is a punishment
For another, as the son's life for the father's.
But that concerns the secondary characters.
It is a fragmentary tragedy
Within the universal whole. The son
And the father alike and equally are spent,
Each one, by the necessity of being
Himself, the unalterable necessity
Of being this unalterable animal.
This force of nature in action is the major
Tragedy. This is destiny unperplexed,
The happiest enemy. And it may be
That in his Mediterranean cloister a man,
Reclining, eased of desire, establishes
The visible, a zone of blue and orange
Versicolorings, establishes a time
To watch the fire-feinting sea and calls it good,
The ultimate good, sure of a reality
Of the longest meditation, the maximum,
The assassin's scene. Evil in evil is
Comparative. The assassin discloses himself,
The force that destroys us is disclosed, within
This maximum, an adventure to be endured
With the politest helplessness. Ay-mi!
One feels its action moving in the blood.

XIV

Victor Serge said, 'I followed his argument
With the blank uneasiness which one might feel
In the presence of a logical lunatic.'
He said it of Konstantinov. Revolution
Is the affair of logical lunatics.
The politics of emotion must appear
To be an intellectual structure. The cause

Creates a logic not to be distinguished.
From lunacy . . . One wants to be able to walk
By the lake at Geneva and consider logic:
To think of the logicians in their graves
And of the worlds of logic in their great tombs.
Lakes are more reasonable than oceans. Hence,
A promenade amid the grandeurs of the mind,
By a lake, with clouds like lights among great tombs,
Gives one a blank uneasiness, as if
One might meet Konstantinov, who would interrupt
With his lunacy. He would not be aware of the lake.
He would be the lunatic of one idea
In a world of ideas, who would have all the people
Live, work, suffer and die in that idea
In a world of ideas. He would not be aware of the clouds,
Lighting the martyrs of logic with white fire.
His extreme of logic would be illogical.

xv

The greatest poverty is not to live
In a physical world, to feel that one's desire
Is too difficult to tell from despair. Perhaps,
After death, the non-physical people, in paradise,
Itself non-physical, may, by chance, observe
The green corn gleaming and experience
The minor of what we feel. The adventurer
In humanity has not conceived of a race
Completely physical in a physical world.
The green corn gleams and the metaphysicals
Lie sprawling in majors of the August heat,
The rotund emotions, paradise unknown.

This is the thesis scrivened in delight,
The reverberating psalm, the right chorale.
One might have thought of sight, but who could think
Of what it sees, for all the ill it sees?

Speech found the ear, for all the evil sound,
But the dark italics it could not propound.
And out of what one sees and hears and out
Of what one feels, who could have thought to make
So many selves, so many sensuous worlds,
As if the air, the mid-day air, was swarming
With the metaphysical changes that occur,
Merely in living as and where we live.

The House Was Quiet and the World Was Calm

The house was quiet and the world was calm.
The reader became the book; and summer night

Was like the conscious being of the book.
The house was quiet and the world was calm.

The words were spoken as if there was no book,
Except that the reader leaned above the page,

Wanted to lean, wanted much most to be
The scholar to whom his book is true, to whom

The summer night is like a perfection of thought.
The house was quiet because it had to be.

The quiet was part of the meaning, part of the mind:
The access of perfection to the page.

And the world was calm. The truth in a calm world,
In which there is no other meaning, itself

Is calm, itself is summer and night, itself
Is the reader leaning late and reading there.

The Dove in the Belly

The whole of appearance is a toy. For this,
The dove in the belly builds his nest and coos,

Selah, tempestuous bird. How is it that
The rivers shine and hold their mirrors up,

Like excellence collecting excellence?
How is it that the wooden trees stand up

And live and heap their panniers of green
And hold them round the sultry day? Why should

These mountains being high be, also, bright,
Fetched up with snow that never falls to earth?

And this great esplanade of corn, miles wide,
Is something wished for made effectual

And something more. And the people in costumes,
Though poor, though raggeder than ruin, have that

Within them right for terraces – oh, brave salut!
Deep dove, placate you in your hiddenness.

Credences of Summer

I

Now in midsummer come and all fools slaughtered
And spring's infuriations over and a long way
To the first autumnal inhalations, young broods
Are in the grass, the roses are heavy with a weight
Of fragrance and the mind lays by its trouble.

Now the mind lays by its trouble and considers.
The fidgets of remembrance come to this.
This is the last day of a certain year
Beyond which there is nothing left of time.
It comes to this and the imagination's life.

There is nothing more inscribed nor thought nor felt
And this must comfort the heart's core against
Its false disasters – these fathers standing round,
These mothers touching, speaking, being near,
These lovers waiting in the soft dry grass.

II

Postpone the anatomy of summer, as
The physical pine, the metaphysical pine.
Let's see the very thing and nothing else.
Let's see it with the hottest fire of sight.
Burn everything not part of it to ash.

Trace the gold sun about the whitened sky
Without evasion by a single metaphor.
Look at it in its essential barrenness
And say this, this is the centre that I seek.
Fix it in an eternal foliage

And fill the foliage with arrested peace,
Joy of such permanence, right ignorance

Of change still possible. Exile desire
For what is not. This is the barrenness
Of the fertile thing that can attain no more.

III

It is the natural tower of all the world,
The point of survey, green's green apogee,
But a tower more precious than the view beyond,
A point of survey squatting like a throne,
Axis of everything, green's apogee

And happiest folk-land, mostly marriage-hymns.
It is the mountain on which the tower stands,
It is the final mountain. Here the sun,
Sleepless, inhales his proper air, and rests.
This is the refuge that the end creates.

It is the old man standing on the tower,
Who reads no book. His ruddy ancientness
Absorbs the ruddy summer and is appeased,
By an understanding that fulfils his age,
By a feeling capable of nothing more.

IV

One of the limits of reality
Presents itself in Oley when the hay,
Baked through long days, is piled in mows. It is
A land too ripe for enigmas, too serene.
There the distant fails the clairvoyant eye

And the secondary senses of the ear
Swarm, not with secondary sounds, but choirs,
Not evocations but last choirs, last sounds
With nothing else compounded, carried full,
Pure rhetoric of a language without words.

Things stop in that direction and since they stop
The direction stops and we accept what is
As good. The utmost must be good and is
And is our fortune and honey hived in the trees
And mingling of colors at a festival.

V

One day enriches a year. One woman makes
The rest look down. One man becomes a race,
Lofty like him, like him perpetual.
Or do the other days enrich the one?
And is the queen humble as she seems to be,

The charitable majesty of her whole kin?
The bristling soldier, weather-foxed, who looms
In the sunshine is a filial form and one
Of the land's children, easily born, its flesh,
Not fustian. The more than casual blue

Contains the year and other years and hymns
And people, without souvenir. The day
Enriches the year, not as embellishment.
Stripped of remembrance, it displays its strength –
The youth, the vital son, the heroic power.

VI

The rock cannot be broken. It is the truth.
It rises from land and sea and covers them.
It is a mountain half way green and then,
The other immeasurable half, such rock
As placid air becomes. But it is not

A hermit's truth nor symbol in hermitage.
It is the visible rock, the audible,
The brilliant mercy of a sure repose,
On this present ground, the vividest repose,
Things certain sustaining us in certainty.

It is the rock of summer, the extreme,
A mountain luminous half-way in bloom
And then half way in the extremest light
Of sapphires flashing from the central sky,
As if twelve princes sat before a king.

VII

Far in the woods they sang their unreal songs,
Secure. It was difficult to sing in face
Of the object. The singers had to avert themselves
Or else avert the object. Deep in the woods
They sang of summer in the common fields.

They sang desiring an object that was near,
In face of which desire no longer moved,
Nor made of itself that which it could not find . . .
Three times the concentred self takes hold, three times
The thrice concentred self, having possessed

The object, grips it in savage scrutiny,
Once to make captive, once to subjugate
Or yield to subjugation, once to proclaim
The meaning of the capture, this hard prize,
Fully made, fully apparent, fully found.

VIII

The trumpet of morning blows in the clouds and through
The sky. It is the visible announced,
It is the more than visible, the more
Than sharp, illustrious scene. The trumpet cries
This is the successor of the invisible.

This is its substitute in stratagems
Of the spirit. This, in sight and memory,
Must take its place, as what is possible
Replaces what is not. The resounding cry
Is like ten thousand tumblers tumbling down

To share the day. The trumpet supposes that
A mind exists, aware of division, aware
Of its cry as clarion, its diction's way
As that of a personage in a multitude:
Man's mind grown venerable in the unreal.

IX

Fly low, cock bright, and stop on a bean pole. Let
Your brown breast redden, while you wait for warmth.
With one eye watch the willow, motionless.
The gardener's cat is dead, the gardener gone
And last year's garden grows salacious weeds.

A complex of emotions falls apart,
In an abandoned spot. Soft, civil bird,
The decay that you regard: of the arranged
And of the spirit of the arranged, *douceurs*,
Tristesses, the fund of life and death, suave bush

And polished beast, this complex falls apart.
And on your bean pole, it may be, you detect
Another complex of other emotions, not
So soft, so civil, and you make a sound,
Which is not part of the listener's own sense.

X

The personae of summer play the characters
Of an inhuman author, who meditates
With the gold bugs, in blue meadows, late at night.
He does not hear his characters talk. He sees
Them mottled, in the moodiest costumes,

Of blue and yellow, sky and sun, belted
And knotted, sashed and seamed, half pales of red,
Half pales of green, appropriate habit for
The huge decorum, the manner of the time,
Part of the mottled mood of summer's whole,

In which the characters speak because they want
To speak, the fat, the roseate characters,
Free, for a moment, from malice and sudden cry,
Completed in a completed scene, speaking
Their parts as in a youthful happiness.

Notes Toward a Supreme Fiction
To Henry Church

And for what, except for you, do I feel love?
Do I press the extremest book of the wisest man
Close to me, hidden in me day and night?
In the uncertain light of single, certain truth,
Equal in living changingness to the light
In which I meet you, in which we sit at rest,
For a moment in the central of our being,
The vivid transparence that you bring is peace.

It Must Be Abstract

I

Begin, ephebe, by perceiving the idea
Of this invention, this invented world,
The inconceivable idea of the sun.

You must become an ignorant man again
And see the sun again with an ignorant eye
And see it clearly in the idea of it.

Never suppose an inventing mind as source
Of this idea nor for that mind compose
A voluminous master folded in his fire.

How clean the sun when seen in its idea,
Washed in the remotest cleanliness of a heaven
That has expelled us and our images . . .

The death of one god is the death of all.
Let purple Phoebus lie in umber harvest,
Let Phoebus slumber and die in autumn umber,

Phoebus is dead, ephebe. But Phoebus was
A name for something that never could be named.
There was a project for the sun and is.

There is a project for the sun. The sun
Must bear no name, gold flourisher, but be
In the difficulty of what it is to be.

II

It is the celestial ennui of apartments
That sends us back to the first idea, the quick
Of this invention; and yet so poisonous

Are the ravishments of truth, so fatal to
The truth itself, the first idea becomes
The hermit in a poet's metaphors,

Who comes and goes and comes and goes all day.
May there be an ennui of the first idea?
What else, prodigious scholar, should there be?

The monastic man is an artist. The philosopher
Appoints man's place in music, say, today.
But the priest desires. The philosopher desires.

And not to have is the beginning of desire.
To have what is not is its ancient cycle.
It is desire at the end of winter, when

It observes the effortless weather turning blue
And sees the myosotis on its bush.
Being virile, it hears the calendar hymn.

It knows that what it has is what is not
And throws it away like a thing of another time,
As morning throws off stale moonlight and shabby sleep.

III

The poem refreshes life so that we share,
For a moment, the first idea . . . It satisfies
Belief in an immaculate beginning

And sends us, winged by an unconscious will,
To an immaculate end. We move between these points:
From that ever-early candor to its late plural

And the candor of them is the strong exhilaration
Of what we feel from what we think, of thought
Beating in the heart, as if blood newly came,

An elixir, an excitation, a pure power.
The poem, through candor, brings back a power again
That gives a candid kind to everything.

We say: At night an Arabian in my room,
With his damned hoobla-hoobla-hoobla-how,
Inscribes a primitive astronomy

Across the unscrawled fores the future casts
And throws his stars around the floor. By day
The wood-dove used to chant his hoobla-hoo

And still the grossest iridescence of ocean
Howls hoo and rises and howls hoo and falls.
Life's nonsense pierces us with strange relation.

IV

The first idea was not our own. Adam
In Eden was the father of Descartes
And Eve made air the mirror of herself,

Of her sons and of her daughters. They found themselves
In heaven as in glass; a second earth;
And in the earth itself they found a green –

The inhabitants of a very varnished green.
But the first idea was not to shape the clouds
In imitation. The clouds preceded us.

There was a muddy centre before we breathed.
There was a myth before the myth began,
Venerable and articulate and complete.

From this the poem springs: that we live in a place
That is not our own and, much more, not ourselves
And hard it is in spite of blazoned days.

We are the mimics. Clouds are pedagogues.
The air is not a mirror but bare board,
Coulisse bright-dark, tragic chiaroscuro

And comic color of the rose, in which
Abysmal instruments make sounds like pips
Of the sweeping meanings that we add to them.

v

The lion roars at the enraging desert,
Reddens the sand with his red-colored noise,
Defies red emptiness to evolve his match,

Master by foot and jaws and by the mane,
Most supple challenger. The elephant
Breaches the darkness of Ceylon with blares,

The glitter-goes on surfaces of tanks,
Shattering velvetest far-away. The bear,
The ponderous cinnamon, snarls in his mountain

At summer thunder and sleeps through winter snow.
But you, ephebe, look from your attic window,
Your mansard with a rented piano. You lie

In silence upon your bed. You clutch the corner
Of the pillow in your hand. You writhe and press
A bitter utterance from your writhing, dumb,

Yet voluble of dumb violence. You look
Across the roofs as sigil and as ward
And in your centre mark them and are cowed . . .

These are the heroic children whom time breeds
Against the first idea – to lash the lion,
Caparison elephants, teach bears to juggle.

VI

Not to be realized because not to
Be seen, not to be loved nor hated because
Not to be realized. Weather by Franz Hals,

Brushed up by brushy winds in brushy clouds,
Wetted by blue, colder for white. Not to
Be spoken to, without a roof, without

First fruits, without the virginal of birds,
The dark-blown ceinture loosened, not relinquished.
Gay is, gay was, the gay forsythia

And yellow, yellow thins the Northern blue.
Without a name and nothing to be desired,
If only imagined but imagined well.

My house has changed a little in the sun.
The fragrance of the magnolias comes close,
False flick, false form, but falseness close to kin.

It must be visible or invisible,
Invisible or visible or both:
A seeing and unseeing in the eye.

The weather and the giant of the weather,
Say the weather, the mere weather, the mere air:
An abstraction blooded, as a man by thought.

VII

It feels good as it is without the giant,
A thinker of the first idea. Perhaps
The truth depends on a walk around a lake,

A composing as the body tires, a stop
To see hepatica, a stop to watch
A definition growing certain and

A wait within that certainty, a rest
In the swags of pine-trees bordering the lake.
Perhaps there are times of inherent excellence,

As when the cock crows on the left and all
Is well, incalculable balances,
At which a kind of Swiss perfection comes

And a familiar music of the machine
Sets up its Schwärmerei, not balances
That we achieve but balances that happen,

As a man and woman meet and love forthwith.
Perhaps there are moments of awakening,
Extreme, fortuitous, personal, in which

We more than awaken, sit on the edge of sleep,
As on an elevation, and behold
The academies like structures in a mist.

VIII

Can we compose a castle-fortress-home,
Even with the help of Viollet-le-Duc,
And set the MacCullough there as major man?

The first idea is an imagined thing.
The pensive giant prone in violet space
May be the MacCullough, an expedient,

Logos and logic, crystal hypothesis,
Incipit and a form to speak the word
And every latent double in the word,

Beau linguist. But the MacCullough is MacCullough.
It does not follow that major man is man.
If MacCullough himself lay lounging by the sea,

Drowned in its washes, reading in the sound,
About the thinker of the first idea,
He might take habit, whether from wave or phrase,

Or power of the wave, or deepened speech,
Or a leaner being, moving in on him,
Of greater aptitude and apprehension,

As if the waves at last were never broken,
As if the language suddenly, with ease,
Said things it had laboriously spoken.

IX

The romantic intoning, the declaimed clairvoyance
Are parts of apotheosis, appropriate
And of its nature, the idiom thereof.

They differ from reason's click-clack, its applied
Enflashings. But apotheosis is not
The origin of the major man. He comes,

Compact in invincible foils, from reason,
Lighted at midnight by the studious eye,
Swaddled in revery, the object of

The hum of thoughts evaded in the mind,
Hidden from other thoughts, he that reposes
On a breast forever precious for that touch,

For whom the good of April falls tenderly,
Falls down, the cock-birds calling at the time.
My dame, sing for this person accurate songs.

He is and may be but oh! he is, he is,
This foundling of the infected past, so bright,
So moving in the manner of his hand.

Yet look not at his colored eyes. Give him
No names. Dismiss him from your images.
The hot of him is purest in the heart.

X

The major abstraction is the idea of man
And major man is its exponent, abler
In the abstract than in his singular,

More fecund as principle than particle,
Happy fecundity, flor-abundant force,
In being more than an exception, part,

Though an heroic part, of the commonal.
The major abstraction is the commonal,
The inanimate, difficult visage. Who is it?

What rabbi, grown furious with human wish,
What chieftain, walking by himself, crying
Most miserable, most victorious,

Does not see these separate figures one by one,
And yet see only one, in his old coat,
His slouching pantaloons, beyond the town,

Looking for what was, where it used to be?
Cloudless the morning. It is he. The man
In that old coat, those sagging pantaloons,

It is of him, ephebe, to make, to confect
The final elegance, not to console
Nor sanctify, but plainly to propound.

It Must Change

I

The old seraph, parcel-gilded, among violets
Inhaled the appointed odor, while the doves
Rose up like phantoms from chronologies.

The Italian girls wore jonquils in their hair
And these the seraph saw, had seen long since,
In the bandeaux of the mothers, would see again.

The bees came booming as if they had never gone,
As if hyacinths had never gone. We say
This changes and that changes. Thus the constant

Violets, doves, girls, bees and hyacinths
Are inconstant objects of inconstant cause
In a universe of inconstancy. This means

Night-blue is an inconstant thing. The seraph
Is satyr in Saturn, according to his thoughts.
It means the distaste we feel for this withered scene

Is that it has not changed enough. It remains,
It is a repetition. The bees come booming
As if – The pigeons clatter in the air.

An erotic perfume, half of the body, half
Of an obvious acid is sure what it intends
And the booming is blunt, not broken in subtleties.

II

The President ordains the bee to be
Immortal. The President ordains. But does
The body lift its heavy wing, take up,

Again, an inexhaustible being, rise
Over the loftiest antagonist
To drone the green phrases of its juvenal?

Why should the bee recapture a lost blague,
Find a deep echo in a horn and buzz
The bottomless trophy, new hornsman after old?

The President has apples on the table
And barefoot servants round him, who adjust
The curtains to a metaphysical t

And the banners of the nation flutter, burst
On the flag-poles in a red-blue dazzle, whack
At the halyards. Why, then, when in golden fury

Spring vanishes the scraps of winter, why
Should there be a question of returning or
Of death in memory's dream? Is spring a sleep?

This warmth is for lovers at last accomplishing
Their love, this beginning, not resuming, this
Booming and booming of the new-come bee.

III

The great statue of the General Du Puy
Rested immobile, though neighboring catafalques
Bore off the residents of its noble Place.

The right, uplifted foreleg of the horse
Suggested that, at the final funeral,
The music halted and the horse stood still.

On Sundays, lawyers in their promenades
Approached this strongly-heightened effigy
To study the past, and doctors, having bathed

Themselves with care, sought out the nerveless frame
Of a suspension, a permanence, so rigid
That it made the General a bit absurd,

Changed his true flesh to an inhuman bronze.
There never had been, never could be, such
A man. The lawyers disbelieved, the doctors

Said that as keen, illustrious ornament,
As a setting for geraniums, the General,
The very Place Du Puy, in fact, belonged

Among our more vestigial states of mind.
Nothing had happened because nothing had changed.
Yet the General was rubbish in the end.

IV

Two things of opposite natures seem to depend
On one another, as a man depends
On a woman, day on night, the imagined

On the real. This is the origin of change.
Winter and spring, cold copulars, embrace
And forth the particulars of rapture come.

Music falls on the silence like a sense,
A passion that we feel, not understand.
Morning and afternoon are clasped together

And North and South are an intrinsic couple
And sun and rain a plural, like two lovers
That walk away as one in the greenest body.

In solitude the trumpets of solitude
Are not of another solitude resounding;
A little string speaks for a crowd of voices.

The partaker partakes of that which changes him.
The child that touches takes character from the thing,
The body, it touches. The captain and his men

Are one and the sailor and the sea are one.
Follow after, O my companion, my fellow, my self,
Sister and solace, brother and delight.

v

On a blue island in a sky-wide water
The wild orange trees continued to bloom and to bear,
Long after the planter's death. A few limes remained,

Where his house had fallen, three scraggy trees weighted
With garbled green. These were the planter's turquoise
And his orange blotches, these were his zero green,

A green baked greener in the greenest sun.
These were his beaches, his sea-myrtles in
White sand, his patter of the long sea-slushes.

There was an island beyond him on which rested,
An island to the South, on which rested like
A mountain, a pine-apple pungent as Cuban summer.

And là-bas, là-bas, the cool bananas grew,
Hung heavily on the great banana tree,
Which pierces clouds and bends on half the world.

He thought often of the land from which he came,
How that whole country was a melon, pink
If seen rightly and yet a possible red.

An unaffected man in a negative light
Could not have borne his labor nor have died
Sighing that he should leave the banjo's twang.

VI

Bethou me, said sparrow, to the crackled blade,
And you, and you, bethou me as you blow,
When in my coppice you behold me be.

Ah, ké! the bloody wren, the felon jay,
Ké-ké, the jug-throated robin pouring out,
Bethou, bethou, bethou me in my glade.

There was such idiot minstrelsy in rain,
So many clappers going without bells,
That these bethous compose a heavenly gong.

One voice repeating, one tireless chorister,
The phrases of a single phrase, ké-ké,
A single text, granite monotony,

One sole face, like a photograph of fate,
Glass-blower's destiny, bloodless episcopus,
Eye without lid, mind without any dream –

These are of minstrels lacking minstrelsy,
Of an earth in which the first leaf is the tale
Of leaves, in which the sparrow is a bird

Of stone, that never changes. Bethou him, you
And you, bethou him and bethou. It is
A sound like any other. It will end.

VII

After a lustre of the moon, we say
We have not the need of any paradise,
We have not the need of any seducing hymn.

It is true. Tonight the lilacs magnify
The easy passion, the ever-ready love
Of the lover that lies within us and we breathe

An odor evoking nothing, absolute.
We encounter in the dead middle of the night
The purple odor, the abundant bloom.

The lover sighs as for accessible bliss,
Which he can take within him on his breath,
Possess in his heart, conceal and nothing known.

For easy passion and ever-ready love
Are of our earthy birth and here and now
And where we live and everywhere we live,

As in the top-cloud of a May night-evening,
As in the courage of the ignorant man,
Who chants by book, in the heat of the scholar, who writes

The book, hot for another accessible bliss:
The fluctuations of certainty, the change
Of degrees of perception in the scholar's dark.

VIII

On her trip around the world, Nanzia Nunzio
Confronted Ozymandias. She went
Alone and like a vestal long-prepared.

I am the spouse. She took her necklace off
And laid it in the sand. As I am, I am
The spouse. She opened her stone-studded belt.

I am the spouse, divested of bright gold,
The spouse beyond emerald or amethyst,
Beyond the burning body that I bear.

I am the woman stripped more nakedly
Than nakedness, standing before an inflexible
Order, saying I am the contemplated spouse.

Speak to me that, which spoken, will array me
In its own only precious ornament.
Set on me the spirit's diamond coronal.

Clothe me entire in the final filament,
So that I tremble with such love so known
And myself am precious for your perfecting.

Then Ozymandias said the spouse, the bride
Is never naked. A fictive covering
Weaves always glistening from the heart and mind.

IX

The poem goes from the poet's gibberish to
The gibberish of the vulgate and back again.
Does it move to and fro or is it of both

At once? Is it a luminous flittering
Or the concentration of a cloudy day?
Is there a poem that never reaches words

And one that chaffers the time away?
Is the poem both peculiar and general?
There's a meditation there, in which there seems

To be an evasion, a thing not apprehended or
Not apprehended well. Does the poet
Evade us, as in a senseless element?

Evade, this hot, dependent orator,
The spokesman at our bluntest barriers,
Exponent by a form of speech, the speaker

Of a speech only a little of the tongue?
It is the gibberish of the vulgate that he seeks.
He tries by a peculiar speech to speak

The peculiar potency of the general,
To compound the imagination's Latin with
The lingua franca et jocundissima.

A bench was his catalepsy, Theatre
Of Trope. He sat in the park. The water of
The lake was full of artificial things,

Like a page of music, like an upper air,
Like a momentary color, in which swans
Were seraphs, were saints, were changing essences.

The west wind was the music, the motion, the force
To which the swans curveted, a will to change,
A will to make iris frettings on the blank.

There was a will to change, a necessitous
And present way, a presentation, a kind
Of volatile world, too constant to be denied,

The eye of a vagabond in metaphor
That catches our own. The casual is not
Enough. The freshness of transformation is

The freshness of a world. It is our own,
It is ourselves, the freshness of ourselves,
And that necessity and that presentation

Are rubbings of a glass in which we peer.
Of these beginnings, gay and green, propose
The suitable amours. Time will write them down.

It Must Give Pleasure

I

To sing jubilas at exact, accustomed times,
To be crested and wear the mane of a multitude
And so, as part, to exult with its great throat,

To speak of joy and to sing of it, borne on
The shoulders of joyous men, to feel the heart
That is the common, the bravest fundament,

This is a facile exercise. Jerome
Begat the tubas and the fire-wind strings,
The golden fingers picking dark-blue air:

For companies of voices moving there,
To find of sound the bleakest ancestor,
To find of light a music issuing

Whereon it falls in more than sensual mode.
But the difficultest rigor is forthwith,
On the image of what we see, to catch from that

Irrational moment its unreasoning,
As when the sun comes rising, when the sea
Clears deeply, when the moon hangs on the wall

Of heaven-haven. These are not things transformed.
Yet we are shaken by them as if they were.
We reason about them with a later reason.

II

The blue woman, linked and lacquered, at her window
Did not desire that feathery argentines
Should be cold silver, neither that frothy clouds

Should foam, be foamy waves, should move like them,
Nor that the sexual blossoms should repose
Without their fierce addictions, nor that the heat

Of summer, growing fragrant in the night,
Should strengthen her abortive dreams and take
In sleep its natural form. It was enough

For her that she remembered: the argentines
Of spring come to their places in the grape leaves
To cool their ruddy pulses; the frothy clouds

Are nothing but frothy clouds; the frothy blooms
Waste without puberty; and afterward,
When the harmonious heat of August pines

Enters the room, it drowses and is the night.
It was enough for her that she remembered.
The blue woman looked and from her window named

The corals of the dogwood, cold and clear,
Cold, coldly delineating, being real,
Clear and, except for the eye, without intrusion.

III

A lasting visage in a lasting bush,
A face of stone in an unending red,
Red-emerald, red-slitted-blue, a face of slate,

An ancient forehead hung with heavy hair,
The channel slots of rain, the red-rose-red
And weathered and the ruby-water-worn,

The vines around the throat, the shapeless lips,
The frown like serpents basking on the brow,
The spent feeling leaving nothing of itself,

Red-in-red repetitions never going
Away, a little rusty, a little rouged,
A little roughened and ruder, a crown

The eye could not escape, a red renown
Blowing itself upon the tedious ear.
An effulgence faded, dull cornelian

Too venerably used. That might have been.
It might and might have been. But as it was,
A dead shepherd brought tremendous chords from hell

And bade the sheep carouse. Or so they said.
Children in love with them brought early flowers
And scattered them about, no two alike.

We reason of these things with later reason
And we make of what we see, what we see clearly
And have seen, a place dependent on ourselves.

There was a mystic marriage in Catawba,
At noon it was on the mid-day of the year
Between a great captain and the maiden Bawda.

This was their ceremonial hymn: Anon
We loved but would no marriage make. Anon
The one refused the other one to take,

Foreswore the sipping of the marriage wine.
Each must the other take not for his high,
His puissant front nor for her subtle sound,

The shoo-shoo-shoo of secret cymbals round.
Each must the other take as sign, short sign
To stop the whirlwind, balk the elements.

The great captain loved the ever-hill Catawba
And therefore married Bawda, whom he found there,
And Bawda loved the captain as she loved the sun.

They married well because the marriage-place
Was what they loved. It was neither heaven nor hell.
They were love's characters come face to face.

V

We drank Meursault, ate lobster Bombay with mango
Chutney. Then the Canon Aspirin declaimed
Of his sister, in what a sensible ecstasy

She lived in her house. She had two daughters, one
Of four, and one of seven, whom she dressed
The way a painter of pauvred color paints.

But still she painted them, appropriate to
Their poverty, a gray-blue yellowed out
With ribbon, a rigid statement of them, white,

With Sunday pearls, her window's gayety.
She hid them under simple names. She held
Them closelier to her by rejecting dreams.

The words they spoke were voices that she heard.
She looked at them and saw them as they were
And what she felt fought off the barest phrase.

The Canon Aspirin, having said these things,
Reflected, humming an outline of a fugue
Of praise, a conjugation done by choirs.

Yet when her children slept, his sister herself
Demanded of sleep, in the excitements of silence
Only the unmuddled self of sleep, for them.

VI

When at long midnight the Canon came to sleep
And normal things had yawned themselves away,
The nothingness was a nakedness, a point,

Beyond which fact could not progress as fact.
Thereon the learning of the man conceived
Once more night's pale illuminations, gold

Beneath, far underneath, the surface of
His eye and audible in the mountain of
His ear, the very material of his mind.

So that he was the ascending wings he saw
And moved on them in orbits' outer stars
Descending to the children's bed, on which

They lay. Forth then with huge pathetic force
Straight to the utmost crown of night he flew.
The nothingness was a nakedness, a point

Beyond which thought could not progress as thought.
He had to choose. But it was not a choice
Between excluding things. It was not a choice

Between, but of. He chose to include the things
That in each other are included, the whole,
The complicate, the amassing harmony.

VII

He imposes orders as he thinks of them,
As the fox and snake do. It is a brave affair.
Next he builds capitols and in their corridors,

Whiter than wax, sonorous, fame as it is,
He establishes statues of reasonable men,
Who surpassed the most literate owl, the most erudite
Of elephants. But to impose is not
To discover. To discover an order as of
A season, to discover summer and know it,

To discover winter and know it well, to find,
Not to impose, not to have reasoned at all,
Out of nothing to have come on major weather,

It is possible, possible, possible. It must
Be possible. It must be that in time
The real will from its crude compoundings come,

Seeming, at first, a beast disgorged, unlike,
Warmed by a desperate milk. To find the real,
To be stripped of every fiction except one,

The fiction of an absolute – Angel,
Be silent in your luminous cloud and hear
The luminous melody of proper sound.

VIII

What am I to believe? If the angel in his cloud,
Serenely gazing at the violet abyss,
Plucks on his strings to pluck abysmal glory,

Leaps downward through evening's revelations, and
On his spredden wings, needs nothing but deep space,
Forgets the gold centre, the golden destiny,

Grows warm in the motionless motion of his flight,
Am I that imagine this angel less-satisfied?
Are the wings his, the lapis-haunted air?

Is it he or is it I that experience this?
Is it I then that keep saying there is an hour
Filled with expressible bliss, in which I have

No need, am happy, forget need's golden hand,
Am satisfied without solacing majesty,
And if there is an hour there is a day,

There is a month, a year, there is a time
In which majesty is a mirror of the self:
I have not but I am and as I am, I am.

These external regions, what do we fill them with
Except reflections, the escapades of death,
Cinderella fulfilling herself beneath the roof?

IX

Whistle aloud, too weedy wren. I can
Do all that angels can. I enjoy like them,
Like men besides, like men in light secluded,

Enjoying angels. Whistle, forced bugler,
That bugles for the mate, nearby the nest,
Cock bugler, whistle and bugle and stop just short,

Red robin, stop in your preludes, practicing
Mere repetitions. These things at least comprise
An occupation, an exercise, a work,

A thing final in itself and, therefore, good:
One of the vast repetitions final in
Themselves and, therefore, good, the going round

And round and round, the merely going round,
Until merely going round is a final good,
The way wine comes at a table in a wood.

And we enjoy like men, the way a leaf
Above the table spins its constant spin,
So that we look at it with pleasure, look

At it spinning its eccentric measure. Perhaps,
The man-hero is not the exceptional monster,
But he that of repetition is most master.

x

Fat girl, terrestrial, my summer, my night,
How is it I find you in difference, see you there
In a moving contour, a change not quite completed?

You are familiar yet an aberration.
Civil, madam, I am, but underneath
A tree, this unprovoked sensation requires

That I should name you flatly, waste no words,
Check your evasions, hold you to yourself.
Even so when I think of you as strong or tired,

Bent over work, anxious, content, alone,
You remain the more than natural figure. You
Become the soft-footed phantom, the irrational

Distortion, however fragrant, however dear.
That's it: the more than rational distortion,
The fiction that results from feeling. Yes, that.

They will get it straight one day at the Sorbonne.
We shall return at twilight from the lecture
Pleased that the irrational is rational,

Until flicked by feeling, in a gildered street,
I call you by name, my green, my fluent mundo.
You will have stopped revolving except in crystal.

Soldier, there is a war between the mind
And sky, between thought and day and night. It is
For that the poet is always in the sun,

Patches the moon together in his room
To his Virgilian cadences, up down,
Up down. It is a war that never ends.

Yet it depends on yours. The two are one.
They are a plural, a right and left, a pair,
Two parallels that meet if only in

The meeting of their shadows or that meet
In a book in a barrack, a letter from Malay.
But your war ends. And after it you return
With six meats and twelve wines or else without
To walk another room . . . Monsieur and comrade,
The soldier is poor without the poet's lines,

His petty syllabi, the sounds that stick,
Inevitably modulating, in the blood.
And war for war, each has its gallant kind.

How simply the fictive hero becomes the real;
How gladly with proper words the soldier dies,
If he must, or lives on the bread of faithful speech.

What We See Is What We Think

At twelve, the disintegration of afternoon
Began, the return to phantomerei, if not
To phantoms. Till then, it had been the other way:

One imagined the violet trees but the trees stood green,
At twelve, as green as ever they would be.
The sky was blue beyond the vaultiest phrase.

Twelve meant as much as: the end of normal time,
Straight up, an élan without harrowing,
The imprescriptible zenith, free of harangue,

Twelve and the first gray second after, a kind
Of violet gray, a green violet, a thread
To weave a shadow's leg or sleeve, a scrawl

On the pedestal, an ambitious page dog-eared
At the upper right, a pyramid with one side
Like a spectral cut in its perception, a tilt

And its tawny caricature and tawny life,
Another thought, the paramount ado . . .
Since what we think is never what we see.

An Ordinary Evening in New Haven

I

The eye's plain version is a thing apart,
The vulgate of experience. Of this,
A few words, an and yet, and yet, and yet –

As part of the never-ending meditation,
Part of the question that is a giant himself:
Of what is this house composed if not of the sun,

These houses, these difficult objects, dilapidate
Appearances of what appearances,
Words, lines, not meanings, not communications,

Dark things without a double, after all,
Unless a second giant kills the first –
A recent imagining of reality,

Much like a new resemblance of the sun,
Down-pouring, up-springing and inevitable,
A larger poem for a larger audience,

As if the crude collops came together as one,
A mythological form, a festival sphere,
A great bosom, beard and being, alive with age.

II

Suppose these houses are composed of ourselves,
So that they become an impalpable town, full of
Impalpable bells, transparencies of sound,

Sounding in transparent dwellings of the self,
Impalpable habitations that seem to move
In the movement of the colors of the mind,

The far-fire flowing and the dim-coned bells
Coming together in a sense in which we are poised,
Without regard to time or where we are,

In the perpetual reference, object
Of the perpetual meditation, point
Of the enduring, visionary love,

Obscure, in colors whether of the sun
Or mind, uncertain in the clearest bells,
The spirit's speeches, the indefinite,

Confused illuminations and sonorities,
So much ourselves, we cannot tell apart
The idea and the bearer-being of the idea.

III

The point of vision and desire are the same.
It is to the hero of midnight that we pray
On a hill of stones to make beau mont thereof.

If it is misery that infuriates our love,
If the black of night stands glistening on beau mont,
Then, ancientest saint ablaze with ancientest truth,

Say next to holiness is the will thereto,
And next to love is the desire for love,
The desire for its celestial ease in the heart,

Which nothing can frustrate, that most secure,
Unlike love in possession of that which was
To be possessed and is. But this cannot

Possess. It is desire, set deep in the eye,
Behind all actual seeing, in the actual scene,
In the street, in a room, on a carpet or a wall,

Always in emptiness that would be filled,
In denial that cannot contain its blood,
A porcelain, as yet in the bats thereof.

The plainness of plain things is savagery,
As: the last plainness of a man who has fought
Against illusion and was, in a great grinding

Of growling teeth, and falls at night, snuffed out
By the obese opiates of sleep. Plain men in plain towns
Are not precise about the appeasement they need.

They only know a savage assuagement cries
With a savage voice; and in that cry they hear
Themselves transposed, muted and comforted

In a savage and subtle and simple harmony,
A matching and mating of surprised accords,
A responding to a diviner opposite.

So lewd spring comes from winter's chastity.
So, after summer, in the autumn air,
Comes the cold volume of forgotten ghosts,

But soothingly, with pleasant instruments,
So that this cold, a children's tale of ice,
Seems like a sheen of heat romanticized.

V

Inescapable romance, inescapable choice
Of dreams, disillusion as the last illusion,
Reality as a thing seen by the mind,

Not that which is but that which is apprehended,
A mirror, a lake of reflections in a room,
A glassy ocean lying at the door,

A great town hanging pendent in a shade,
An enormous nation happy in a style,
Everything as unreal as real can be,

In the inexquisite eye. Why, then, inquire
Who has divided the world, what entrepreneur?
No man. The self, the chrysalis of all men

Became divided in the leisure of blue day
And more, in branchings after day. One part
Held fast tenaciously in common earth

And one from central earth to central sky
And in moonlit extensions of them in the mind
Searched out such majesty as it could find.

VI

Reality is the beginning not the end,
Naked Alpha, not the hierophant Omega,
Of dense investiture, with luminous vassals.

It is the infant A standing on infant legs,
Not twisted, stooping, polymathic Z,
He that kneels always on the edge of space

In the pallid perceptions of its distances.
Alpha fears men or else Omega's men
Or else his prolongations of the human.

These characters are around us in the scene.
For one it is enough; for one it is not;
For neither is it profound absentia,

Since both alike appoint themselves the choice
Custodians of the glory of the scene,
The immaculate interpreters of life.

But that's the difference: in the end and the way
To the end. Alpha continues to begin.
Omega is refreshed at every end.

VII

In the presence of such chapels and such schools,
The impoverished architects appear to be
Much richer, more fecund, sportive and alive.

The objects tingle and the spectator moves
With the objects. But the spectator also moves
With lesser things, with things exteriorized

Out of rigid realists. It is as if
Men turning into things, as comedy,
Stood, dressed in antic symbols, to display

The truth about themselves, having lost, as things,
That power to conceal they had as men,
Not merely as to depth but as to height

As well, not merely as to the commonplace
But, also, as to their miraculous,
Conceptions of new mornings of new worlds,

The tips of cock-cry pinked out pastily,
As that which was incredible becomes,
In misted contours, credible day again.

VIII

We fling ourselves, constantly longing, on this form.
We descend to the street and inhale a health of air
To our sepulchral hollows. Love of the real

Is soft in three-four cornered fragrances
From five-six cornered leaves, and green, the signal
To the lover, and blue, as of a secret place

In the anonymous color of the universe.
Our breath is like a desperate element
That we must calm, the origin of a mother tongue

With which to speak to her, the capable
In the midst of foreignness, the syllable
Of recognition, avowal, impassioned cry,

The cry that contains its converse in itself,
In which looks and feelings mingle and are part
As a quick answer modifies a question,

Not wholly spoken in a conversation between
Two bodies disembodied in their talk,
Too fragile, too immediate for any speech.

IX

We keep coming back and coming back
To the real: to the hotel instead of the hymns
That fall upon it out of the wind. We seek

The poem of pure reality, untouched
By trope or deviation, straight to the word,
Straight to the transfixing object, to the object

At the exactest point at which it is itself,
Transfixing by being purely what it is,
A view of New Haven, say, through the certain eye,

The eye made clear of uncertainty, with the sight
Of simple seeing, without reflection. We seek
Nothing beyond reality. Within it,

Everything, the spirit's alchemicana
Included, the spirit that goes roundabout
And through included, not merely the visible,

The solid, but the movable, the moment,
The coming on of feasts and the habits of saints,
The pattern of the heavens and high, night air.

X

It is fatal in the moon and empty there.
But, here, allons. The enigmatical
Beauty of each beautiful enigma

Becomes amassed in a total double-thing.
We do not know what is real and what is not.
We say of the moon, it is haunted by the man

Of bronze whose mind was made up and who, therefore, died.
We are not men of bronze and we are not dead.
His spirit is imprisoned in constant change.

But ours is not imprisoned. It resides
In a permanence composed of impermanence,
In a faithfulness as against the lunar light,

So that morning and evening are like promises kept,
So that the approaching sun and its arrival,
Its evening feast and the following festival,

This faithfulness of reality, this mode,
This tendance and venerable holding-in
Make gay the hallucinations in surfaces.

XI

In the metaphysical streets of the physical town
We remember the lion of Juda and we save
The phrase . . . Say of each lion of the spirit

It is a cat of a sleek transparency
That shines with a nocturnal shine alone.
The great cat must stand potent in the sun.

The phrase grows weak. The fact takes up the strength
Of the phrase. It contrives the self-same evocations
And Juda becomes New Haven or else must.

In the metaphysical streets, the profoundest forms
Go with the walker subtly walking there.
These he destroys with wafts of wakening,

Free from their majesty and yet in need
Of majesty, of an invincible clou,
A minimum of making in the mind,

A verity of the most veracious men,
The propounding of four seasons and twelve months,
The brilliancy at the central of the earth.

XII

The poem is the cry of its occasion,
Part of the res itself and not about it.
The poet speaks the poem as it is,

Not as it was: part of the reverberation
Of a windy night as it is, when the marble statues
Are like newspapers blown by the wind. He speaks

By sight and insight as they are. There is no
Tomorrow for him. The wind will have passed by,
The statues will have gone back to be things about.

The mobile and the immobile flickering
In the area between is and was are leaves,
Leaves burnished in autumnal burnished trees

And leaves in whirlings in the gutters, whirlings
Around and away, resembling the presence of thought,
Resembling the presences of thoughts, as if,

In the end, in the whole psychology, the self,
The town, the weather, in a casual litter,
Together, said words of the world are the life of the world.

XIII

The ephebe is solitary in his walk.
He skips the journalism of subjects, seeks out
The perquisites of sanctity, enjoys

A strong mind in a weak neighborhood and is
A serious man without the serious,
Inactive in his singular respect.

He is neither priest nor proctor at low eve,
Under the birds, among the perilous owls,
In the big X of the returning primitive.

It is a fresh spiritual that he defines,
A coldness in a long, too-constant warmth,
A thing on the side of a house, not deep in a cloud,

A difficulty that we predicate:
The difficulty of the visible
To the nations of the clear invisible,

The actual landscape with its actual horns
Of baker and butcher blowing, as if to hear,
Hear hard, gets at an essential integrity.

XIV

The dry eucalyptus seeks god in the rainy cloud.
Professor Eucalyptus of New Haven seeks him
In New Haven with an eye that does not look

Beyond the object. He sits in his room, beside
The window, close to the ramshackle spout in which
The rain falls with a ramshackle sound. He seeks

God in the object itself, without much choice.
It is a choice of the commodious adjective
For what he sees, it comes in the end to that:

The description that makes it divinity, still speech
As it touches the point of reverberation – not grim
Reality but reality grimly seen

And spoken in paradisal parlance new
And in any case never grim, the human grim
That is part of the indifference of the eye

Indifferent to what it sees. The tink-tonk
Of the rain in the spout is not a substitute.
It is of the essence not yet well perceived.

XV

He preserves himself against the repugnant rain
By an instinct for a rainless land, the self
Of his self, come at upon wide delvings of wings.

The instinct for heaven had its counterpart:
The instinct for earth, for New Haven, for his room,
The gay tournamonde as of a single world

In which he is and as and is are one.
For its counterpart a kind of counterpoint
Irked the wet wallows of the water-spout.

The rain kept falling loudly in the trees
And on the ground. The hibernal dark that hung
In primavera, the shadow of bare rock,

Becomes the rock of autumn, glittering,
Ponderable source of each imponderable,
The weight we lift with the finger of a dream,

The heaviness we lighten by light will,
By the hand of desire, faint, sensitive, the soft
Touch and trouble of the touch of the actual hand.

XVI

Among time's images, there is not one
Of this present, the venerable mask above
The dilapidation of dilapidations.

The oldest-newest day is the newest alone.
The oldest-newest night does not creak by,
With lanterns, like a celestial ancientness.

Silently it heaves its youthful sleep from the sea –
The Oklahoman – the Italian blue
Beyond the horizon with its masculine,

Their eyes closed, in a young palaver of lips.
And yet the wind whimpers oldly of old age
In the western night. The venerable mask,

In this perfection, occasionally speaks
And something of death's poverty is heard.
This should be tragedy's most moving face.

It is a bough in the electric light
And exhalations in the eaves, so little
To indicate the total leaflessness.

XVII

The color is almost the color of comedy,
Not quite. It comes to the point and at the point,
It fails. The strength at the center is serious.

Perhaps instead of failing it rejects
As a serious strength rejects pin-idleness.
A blank underlies the trials of device,

The dominant blank, the unapproachable.
This is the mirror of the high serious:
Blue verdured into a damask's lofty symbol,

Gold easings and ouncings and fluctuations of thread
And beetling of belts and lights of general stones,
Like blessed beams from out a blessed bush

Or the wasted figurations of the wastes
Of night, time and the imagination,
Saved and beholden, in a robe of rays.

These fitful sayings are, also, of tragedy:
The serious reflection is composed
Neither of comic nor tragic but of commonplace.

XVIII

It is the window that makes it difficult
To say good-by to the past and to live and to be
In the present state of things as, say, to paint

In the present state of painting and not the state
Of thirty years ago. It is looking out
Of the window and walking in the street and seeing,

As if the eyes were the present or part of it,
As if the ears heard any shocking sound,
As if life and death were ever physical.

The life and death of this carpenter depend
On a fuchsia in a can – and iridescences
Of petals that will never be realized,

hings not yet true which he perceives through truth,
Or thinks he does, as he perceives the present,
Or thinks he does, a carpenter's iridescences,

Wooden, the model for astral apprentices,
A city slapped up like a chest of tools,
The eccentric exterior of which the clocks talk.

XIX

The moon rose in the mind and each thing there
Picked up its radial aspect in the night,
Prostrate below the singleness of its will.

That which was public green turned private gray.
At another time, the radial aspect came
From a different source. But there was always one:

A century in which everything was part
Of that century and of its aspect, a personage,
A man who was the axis of his time,

An image that begot its infantines,
Imaginary poles whose intelligence
Streamed over chaos their civilities.

What is the radial aspect of this place,
This present colony of a colony
Of colonies, a sense in the changing sense

Of things? A figure like Ecclesiast,
Rugged and luminous, chants in the dark
A text that is an answer, although obscure.

xx

The imaginative transcripts were like clouds,
Today; and the transcripts of feeling, impossible
To distinguish. The town was a residuum,

A neuter shedding shapes in an absolute.
Yet the transcripts of it when it was blue remain;
And the shapes that it took in feeling, the persons that

It became, the nameless, flitting characters –
These actors still walk in a twilight muttering lines.
It may be that they mingle, clouds and men, in the air

Or street or about the corners of a man,
Who sits thinking in the corners of a room.
In this chamber the pure sphere escapes the impure,

Because the thinker himself escapes. And yet
To have evaded clouds and men leaves him
A naked being with a naked will

And everything to make. He may evade
Even his own will and in his nakedness
Inhabit the hypnosis of that sphere.

XXI

But he may not. He may not evade his will,
Nor the wills of other men; and he cannot evade
The will of necessity, the will of wills –

Romanza out of the black shepherd's isle,
Like the constant sound of the water of the sea
In the hearing of the shepherd and his black forms;

Out of the isle, but not of any isle.
Close to the senses there lies another isle
And there the senses give and nothing take,

The opposite of Cythère, an isolation
At the center, the object of the will, this place,
The things around – the alternate romanza

Out of the surfaces, the windows, the walls,
The bricks grown brittle in time's poverty,
The clear. A celestial mode is paramount,

If only in the branches sweeping in the rain:
The two romanzas, the distant and the near,
Are a single voice in the boo-ha of the wind.

Professor Eucalyptus said, 'The search
For reality is as momentous as
The search for god.' It is the philosopher's search

For an interior made exterior
And the poet's search for the same exterior made
Interior: breathless things broodingly abreath

With the inhalations of original cold
And of original earliness. Yet the sense
Of cold and earliness is a daily sense,

Not the predicate of bright origin.
Creation is not renewed by images
Of lone wanderers. To re-create, to use

The cold and earliness and bright origin
Is to search. Likewise to say of the evening star,
The most ancient light in the most ancient sky,

That it is wholly an inner light, that it shines
From the sleepy bosom of the real, re-creates,
Searches a possible for its possibleness.

XXIII

The sun is half the world, half everything,
The bodiless half. There is always this bodiless half,
This illumination, this elevation, this future

Or, say, the late going colors of that past,
Effete green, the woman in black cassimere.
If, then, New Haven is half sun, what remains,

At evening, after dark, is the other half,
Lighted by space, big over those that sleep,
Of the single future of night, the single sleep,

As of a long, inevitable sound,
A kind of cozening and coaxing sound,
And the goodness of lying in a maternal sound,

Unfretted by day's separate, several selves,
Being part of everything come together as one.
In this identity, disembodiments

Still keep occurring. What is, uncertainly,
Desire prolongs its adventure to create
Forms of farewell, furtive among green ferns.

The consolations of space are nameless things.
It was after the neurosis of winter. It was
In the genius of summer that they blew up

The statue of Jove among the boomy clouds.
It took all day to quieten the sky
And then to refill its emptiness again,

So that at the edge of afternoon, not over,
Before the thought of evening had occurred
Or the sound of Incomincia had been set,

There was a clearing, a readiness for first bells,
An opening for outpouring, the hand was raised:
There was a willingness not yet composed,

A knowing that something certain had been proposed,
Which, without the statue, would be new,
An escape from repetition, a happening

In space and the self, that touched them both at once
And alike, a point of the sky or of the earth
Or of a town poised at the horizon's dip.

XXV

Life fixed him, wandering on the stair of glass,
With its attentive eyes. And, as he stood,
On his balcony, outsensing distances,

There were looks that caught him out of empty air.
C'est toujours la vie qui me regarde . . . This was
Who watched him, always, for unfaithful thought.

This sat beside his bed, with its guitar,
To keep him from forgetting, without a word,
A note or two disclosing who it was.

Nothing about him ever stayed the same,
Except this hidalgo and his eye and tune,
The shawl across one shoulder and the hat.

The commonplace became a rumpling of blazons.
What was real turned into something most unreal,
Bare beggar-tree, hung low for fruited red

In isolated moments – isolations
Were false. The hidalgo was permanent, abstract,
A hatching that stared and demanded an answering look.

XXVI

How facilely the purple blotches fell
On the walk, purple and blue, and red and gold,
Blooming and beaming and voluming colors out.

Away from them, capes, along the afternoon Sound,
Shook off their dark marine in lapis light.
The sea shivered in transcendent change, rose up

As rain and booming, gleaming, blowing, swept
The wateriness of green wet in the sky.
Mountains appeared with greater eloquence

Than that of their clouds. These lineaments were the earth,
Seen as inamorata, of loving fame
Added and added out of a fame-full heart . . .

But, here, the inamorata, without distance
And thereby lost, and naked or in rags,
Shrunk in the poverty of being close,

Touches, as one hand touches another hand,
Or as a voice that, speaking without form,
Gritting the ear, whispers humane repose.

XXVII

A scholar, in his Segmenta, left a note,
As follows, 'The Ruler of Reality,
If more unreal than New Haven, is not

A real ruler, but rules what is unreal.'
In addition, there were draftings of him, thus:
'He is the consort of the Queen of Fact.

Sunrise is his garment's hem, sunset is hers.
He is the theorist of life, not death,
The total excellence of its total book.'

Again, 'The sibilance of phrases is his
Or partly his. His voice is audible,
As the fore-meaning in music is.' Again,

'This man abolishes by being himself
That which is not ourselves: the regalia,
The attributions, the plume and helmet-ho.'

Again, 'He has thought it out, he thinks it out,
As he has been and is and, with the Queen
Of Fact, lies at his ease beside the sea.'

XXVIII

If it should be true that reality exists
In the mind: the tin plate, the loaf of bread on it,
The long-bladed knife, the little to drink and her

Misericordia, it follows that
Real and unreal are two in one: New Haven
Before and after one arrives or, say,

Bergamo on a postcard, Rome after dark,
Sweden described, Salzburg with shaded eyes
Or Paris in conversation at a café.

This endlessly elaborating poem
Displays the theory of poetry,
As the life of poetry. A more severe,

More harassing master would extemporize
Subtler, more urgent proof that the theory
Of poetry is the theory of life,

As it is, in the intricate evasions of as,
In things seen and unseen, created from nothingness,
The heavens, the hells, the worlds, the longed-for lands.

XXIX

In the land of the lemon trees, yellow and yellow were
Yellow-blue, yellow-green, pungent with citron-sap,
Dangling and spangling, the mic-mac of mocking birds.

In the land of the elm trees, wandering mariners
Looked on big women, whose ruddy-ripe images
Wreathed round and round the round wreath of autumn.

They rolled their r's, there, in the land of the citrons.
In the land of big mariners, the words they spoke
Were mere brown clods, mere catching weeds of talk.

When the mariners came to the land of the lemon trees,
At last, in that blond atmosphere, bronzed hard,
They said, 'We are back once more in the land of the elm
    trees,

But folded over, turned round.' It was the same,
Except for the adjectives, an alteration
Of words that was a change of nature, more

Than the difference that clouds make over a town.
The countrymen were changed and each constant thing.
Their dark-colored words had redescribed the citrons.

XXX

The last leaf that is going to fall has fallen.
The robins are là-bas, the squirrels, in tree-caves,
Huddle together in the knowledge of squirrels.

The wind has blown the silence of summer away.
It buzzes beyond the horizon or in the ground:
In mud under ponds, where the sky used to be reflected.

The barrenness that appears is an exposing.
It is not part of what is absent, a halt
For farewells, a sad hanging on for remembrances.

It is a coming on and a coming forth.
The pines that were fans and fragrances emerge,
Staked solidly in a gusty grappling with rocks.

The glass of the air becomes an element –
It was something imagined that has been washed away.
A clearness has returned. It stands restored.

It is not an empty clearness, a bottomless sight.
It is a visibility of thought,
In which hundreds of eyes, in one mind, see at once.

XXXI

The less legible meanings of sounds, the little reds
Not often realized, the lighter words
In the heavy drum of speech, the inner men

Behind the outer shields, the sheets of music
In the strokes of thunder, dead candles at the window
When day comes, fire-foams in the motions of the sea,

Flickings from finikin to fine finikin
And the general fidget from busts of Constantine
To photographs of the late president, Mr Blank,

These are the edgings and inchings of final form,
The swarming activities of the formulae
Of statement, directly and indirectly getting at,

Like an evening evoking the spectrum of violet,
A philosopher practicing scales on his piano,
A woman writing a note and tearing it up.

It is not in the premise that reality
Is a solid. It may be a shade that traverses
A dust, a force that traverses a shade.

A Quiet Normal Life

His place, as he sat and as he thought, was not
In anything that he constructed, so frail,
So barely lit, so shadowed over and naught,

As, for example, a world in which, like snow,
He became an inhabitant, obedient
To gallant notions on the part of cold.

It was here. This was the setting and the time
Of year. Here in his house and in his room,
In his chair, the most tranquil thought grew peaked

And the oldest and the warmest heart was cut
By gallant notions on the part of night –
Both late and alone, above the crickets' chords,

Babbling, each one, the uniqueness of its sound.
There was no fury in transcendent forms.
But his actual candle blazed with artifice.

Final Soliloquy of the Interior Paramour

Light the first light of evening, as in a room
In which we rest and, for small reason, think
The world imagined is the ultimate good.

This is, therefore, the intensest rendezvous.
It is in that thought that we collect ourselves,
Out of all the indifferences, into one thing:

Within a single thing, a single shawl
Wrapped tightly round us, since we are poor, a warmth,
A light, a power, the miraculous influence.

Here, now, we forget each other and ourselves.
We feel the obscurity of an order, a whole,
A knowledge, that which arranged the rendezvous,

Within its vital boundary, in the mind.
We say God and the imagination are one . . .
How high that highest candle lights the dark.

Out of this same light, out of the central mind,
We make a dwelling in the evening air,
In which being there together is enough.

The Rock

It is an illusion that we were ever alive,
Lived in the houses of mothers, arranged ourselves
By our own motions in a freedom of air.

Regard the freedom of seventy years ago.
It is no longer air. The houses still stand,
Though they are rigid in rigid emptiness.

Even our shadows, their shadows, no longer remain.
The lives these lived in the mind are at an end.
They never were . . . The sounds of the guitar

Were not and are not. Absurd. The words spoken
Were not and are not. It is not to be believed.
The meeting at noon at the edge of the field seems like

An invention, an embrace between one desperate clod
And another in a fantastic consciousness,
In a queer assertion of humanity:

A theorem proposed between the two –
Two figures in a nature of the sun,
In the sun's design of its own happiness,

As if nothingness contained a métier,
A vital assumption, an impermanence
In its permanent cold, an illusion so desired

That the green leaves came and covered the high rock,
That the lilacs came and bloomed, like a blindness cleaned,
Exclaiming bright sight, as it was satisfied,

In a birth of sight. The blooming and the musk
Were being alive, an incessant being alive,
A particular of being, that gross universe.

It is not enough to cover the rock with leaves.
We must be cured of it by a cure of the ground
Or a cure of ourselves, that is equal to a cure

Of the ground, a cure beyond forgetfulness.
And yet the leaves, if they broke into bud,
If they broke into bloom, if they bore fruit,

And if we ate the incipient colorings
Of their fresh culls might be a cure of the ground.
The fiction of the leaves is the icon

Of the poem, the figuration of blessedness,
And the icon is the man. The pearled chaplet of spring,
The magnum wreath of summer, time's autumn snood,

Its copy of the sun, these cover the rock.
These leaves are the poem, the icon and the man.
These are a cure of the ground and of ourselves,

In the predicate that there is nothing else.
They bud and bloom and bear their fruit without change.
They are more than leaves that cover the barren rock.

They bud the whitest eye, the pallidest sprout,
New senses in the engenderings of sense,
The desire to be at the end of distances,

The body quickened and the mind in root.
They bloom as a man loves, as he lives in love.
They bear their fruit so that the year is known,

As if its understanding was brown skin,
The honey in its pulp, the final found,
The plenty of the year and of the world.

In this plenty, the poem makes meanings of the rock,
Of such mixed motion and such imagery
That its barrenness becomes a thousand things

And so exists no more. This is the cure
Of leaves and of the ground and of ourselves.
His words are both the icon and the man.

III FORMS OF THE ROCK IN A NIGHT-HYMN

The rock is the gray particular of man's life,
The stone from which he rises, up – and – ho,
The step to the bleaker depths of his descents . . .

The rock is the stern particular of the air,
The mirror of the planets, one by one,
But through man's eye, their silent rhapsodist,

Turquoise the rock, at odious evening bright
With redness that sticks fast to evil dreams;
The difficult rightness of half-risen day.

The rock is the habitation of the whole,
Its strength and measure, that which is near, point A
In a perspective that begins again

At B: the origin of the mango's rind.
It is the rock where tranquil must adduce
Its tranquil self, the main of things, the mind,

The starting point of the human and the end,
That in which space itself is contained, the gate
To the enclosure, day, the things illumined

By day, night and that which night illumines,
Night and its midnight-minting fragrances,
Night's hymn of the rock, as in a vivid sleep.

The Dove in Spring

Brooder, brooder, deep beneath its walls –
A small howling of the dove
Makes something of the little there,

The little and the dark, and that
In which it is and that in which
It is established. There the dove

Makes this small howling, like a thought
That howls in the mind or like a man
Who keeps seeking out his identity

In that which is and is established . . . It howls
Of the great sizes of an outer bush
And the great misery of the doubt of it,

Of stripes of silver that are strips
Like slits across a space, a place
And state of being large and light.

There is this bubbling before the sun,
This howling at one's ear, too far
For daylight and too near for sleep.

The Planet on the Table

Ariel was glad he had written his poems.
They were of a remembered time
Or of something seen that he liked.

Other makings of the sun
Were waste and welter
And the ripe shrub writhed.

His self and the sun were one
And his poems, although makings of his self,
Were no less makings of the sun.

It was not important that they survive.
What mattered was that they should bear
Some lineament or character,

Some aZuence, if only half-perceived,
In the poverty of their words,
Of the planet of which they were part.

Not Ideas About the Thing But the Thing Itself

At the earliest ending of winter,
In March, a scrawny cry from outside
Seemed like a sound in his mind.

He knew that he heard it,
A bird's cry, at daylight or before,
In the early March wind.

With slight, prismatic reeks not recollected,
A bubble without a wall on which to hang.

The curtains, when pulled, might show another whole,
An azure outre-terre, oranged and rosed,
At the elbow of Copernicus, a sphere,
A universe without life's limp and lack,
Philosophers' end . . . What difference would it make,
So long as the mind, for once, fulfilled itself?

Of Mere Being

The palm at the end of the mind,
Beyond the last thought, rises
In the bronze decor,

A gold-feathered bird
Sings in the palm, without human meaning,
Without human feeling, a foreign song.

You know then that it is not the reason
That makes us happy or unhappy.
The bird sings. Its feathers shine.

The palm stands on the edge of space.
The wind moves slowly in the branches.
The bird's fire-fangled feathers dangle down.

A Clear Day and No Memories

No soldiers in the scenery,
No thoughts of people now dead,
As they were fifty years ago,
Young and living in a live air,
Young and walking in the sunshine,
Bending in blue dresses to touch something,
Today the mind is not part of the weather.

Today the air is clear of everything.
It has no knowledge except of nothingness
And it flows over us without meanings,
As if none of us had ever been here before
And are not now: in this shallow spectacle,
This invisible activity, this sense.